NEW DECORATING

NEW DECORATING

WITH STYLISH, PRACTICAL PROJECTS FOR EVERY ROOM

Elizabeth Wilhide and Joanna Copestick

Special photography by Hannah Lewis

 conran OCTOPUS

CONTENTS

First published in 1998 as *Contemporary Decorating*

by Conran Octopus Ltd

a part of Octopus Publishing Group

2–4 Heron Quays, London E14 4JP

www.conran-octopus.co.uk

This paperback edition published in 2003

Commissioning editor	Denny Hemming
Managing editor	Helen Ridge
Copy editor	Sharon Amos
Art editor	Tony Seddon
Stylist for special photography	Sue Parker
Picture research	Rachel Davies
Production	Julia Golding

A catalogue record for this book is available

from the British Library

ISBN 1 84091 330 4

Printed in China

6
•
NEW MODERN

18
•
WALLS

44
•
FLOORS

70
•
WINDOWS
& DOORS

96
•
FURNITURE &
FURNISHINGS

118
•
STORAGE & DISPLAY

140
•
Sources

142
•
Index

144
•
Acknowledgments

NEW MODERN

screens, partitions and built-in features orchestrate space. Simple but not stark, contemporary decorating offers scope for self-expression and creative flair within a well-structured framework attuned to everyday needs.

Now, at the end of the twentieth century, modernity has finally come of age. With origins in the forthright use of materials pioneered by the Arts and Crafts Movement more than a hundred years ago, and the functional honesty of the machine aesthetic of the early decades

Above **In this streamlined yet comfortable bedroom, the soft, neutral colour unites the different planes of walls and ceiling. The oversized headboard also acts as a screen, concealing clothes and clutter.**

Right **Light and space are two of the most important elements in contemporary interiors. Here, natural light from the upper floor floods down an open spiral staircase to merge with light let in through the large windows and reflected off the frosted glass screens.**

It's time to be modern. Sharp and uplifting, comfortable and hard-working, contemporary decorating is economical in everything but spirit. Focusing attention on the basic elements of light, colour, space and texture achieves a new clarity and direction in home design.

Bold planes of tangy colour, clean-cut materials such as moulded plywood, glass brick and zinc sheeting, together with classic contemporary furnishings, create rooms that are comfortable, practical, easy on the eye and easy to maintain. User-friendly storage tames clutter; carefully judged lighting lends atmosphere;

of this century, the modern approach to decoration and design has developed into a mature and progressive style of living.

While pioneers of modernism may have put their case with missionary zeal, contemporary decorating is much more of a broad church. Versatile, adaptable and accommodating, it puts human pleasures and activities back firmly in the centre of the picture where they belong. The object is not to enforce a denial of all the elements that make our surroundings enjoyable

Left **Early 20th-century design classics such as Le Corbusier's chaise longue look as modern today as they did 70 years ago. Clean, functional but also comfortable, this piece of furniture has today acquired cult status.**

– colour, pattern, texture and detail – but to put a fresh face on our homes and bring them up to date with the way we live now. Nor is contemporary decorating a mere fashion statement: it is an outlook that goes beyond the superficial to provide a refreshingly positive background for real living.

It is a paradox of our century that innovation has been so warmly embraced in some spheres of life, but held at arm's length in others. Sweeping technological changes have revolutionized transport, communication and production and transformed our lives in the process; yet all too often over the past hundred years these radical developments have simply not been expressed on home territory. Homes may be equipped with the latest services and technology, but still decorated and furnished according to the conventions of past generations.

Contemporary decorating opens up the home to new and exciting possibilities. Strong colour, characterful texture and clean lines give a clear sense of purpose for functional living – decorating for a new millennium.

THE SHOCK OF THE NEW

Modernism has a past. One of the first shocks the new has to offer is the realization of how old it actually is. Such classic modern designs as Le Corbusier's chaise longue or Marcel Breuer's Cesca chair date back to 1928, while the radical high-backed Hill House chairs of Charles Rennie Mackintosh, first designed in 1901, are even more venerable. Even Scandinavian modern was first modern forty years ago.

Modern designs are now old enough to be collectable, with originals auctioned in sale rooms for serious amounts of money. On a less exalted plane, there is a brisk trade in all kinds of 'contemporary' furnishings and artefacts of the recent past, from 1950s fabric patterned with abstract imagery borrowed from the world of science to see-through inflatable chairs of the space-age 1960s.

All this may seem to indicate that modernism is beginning to show signs of mutating into one more 'period' style or at least a 'retro' one. But this is far from true. What is attractive and refreshing about such modern designs as Jacobsen's Egg chair or Mies van der Rohe's Barcelona chair is their undiminished sense of

newness. And to some extent they have remained new because in many homes the twentieth century has never really arrived.

The reasons for this are not difficult to discover. Modernism must rank as one of the most misinterpreted, least understood and worst-applied theories in the history of design, for a wide variety of factors that range from the trivial to the fundamental. Some critics, for example, have blamed the popular identification of modernism with stark, monochrome interiors on the misconceptions that arose from the fact that many early modernist houses were only known

through the medium of black and white photography. Certainly it came as a surprise to many how colourful the work of architects such as Le Corbusier could be. More damningly, in Britain above all, modernity came to be synonymous with discredited forms of public housing such as high-rises or 'streets in the sky', where shoddy building, cut-price materials and insensitive planning resulted in new urban wastelands. Even in the realm of private housing, the concepts were often applied with little consideration for context. In wet, northern climates, flat roofs leaked, concrete stained and façades merged depressingly with dull grey sky.

Catchphrases have not helped. When 'less is more' appears to point down the blind alley of minimalism or the house as 'a machine for living' can be trivially read as promising a sterile robotic existence, it is not surprising that many people have chosen to shut their doors on the new.

Yet there are strong signs that, at long last, the flight from modernity has moved into reverse. Just as we are about to say goodbye to the century, we are finally beginning to come to terms with some of its more radical developments in the field of design. As we tire of the endless recreations of past styles, the synthetic nostalgia of countrified looks and the sheer clutter and artifice that accompany them, there is an increasing appreciation of what modernity has to offer – seamless planning, flexible arrangement, rich texture, pure form and inspiring colour. All this, together with the positive and optimistic feeling of living in the here and now. Modern, finally, makes sense.

Right **Glass bricks have long been appreciated as building blocks by architects; now they are finally being lauded by a wider audience. Inserted into walls or acting as room dividers in their own right, they screen light, as well as decorate a space.**

THEMES AND INSPIRATION

Decoration often seems to imply a superficial gloss, a titivation of the interior to create merely visual effect. But in modern interiors decor is more than skin deep. In contemporary decorating, the palette is not simply paint colours or fabric swatches, but a whole family of materials, both natural and synthetic, working together in soulful combination to enrich and give depth to the interior. In this idiom, materials are enjoyed for their intrinsic qualities: wood for its grain and contours, metal for its crisp, gleaming edge, glass brick for its mellow translucency.

We owe at least some of our appreciation of materials in their own right to the designers of the Arts and Crafts Movement of the late nineteenth century, who were the first to stress the importance of 'honesty' in material use. In High Victorian style, nothing was ever as it seemed. Stone fireplaces were painted to look like marble, softwood was grained and stained to look like hardwood and the basic forms of tables and chairs were smothered under obliterating layers of fabric, frills and trimming. The Arts and Crafts Movement represented a direct challenge to this status-seeking artifice. In the progressive interiors of these designers there was a real sense of getting back to what was basic and tangible – solid oak, plain whitewash, luminous ceramics. Furnishings were relatively simple, unpretentious and, preferably, hand-crafted in the time-honoured vernacular.

The Arts and Crafts practitioners were not modernists, but they had an important impact on the emerging Modern Movement. By the

early twentieth century, a number of progressive design movements had sprung up all over Europe, culminating in the most influential design school of all: the Bauhaus.

Everyone is familiar with the 'form follows function' credo of these early modernists, who eschewed superficial ornament and archaic reference in the design of objects, furniture, buildings and machines. Translated into the context of the interior, this shifted the emphasis

Above **Marble, concrete, leather and wood blend harmoniously in this spacious, light-filled hallway to create a welcoming atmosphere. With such a rich textural mix, colour is not so essential.**

from the expression of status and tradition to an elemental celebration of light, space and volume.

The students and teachers of the Bauhaus, together with architects and designers such as Le Corbusier and Marcel Breuer, were champions of the machine age, inspired by new materials, advances in technology and mass production. The streamlined form of an aircraft's wing suggested a new vocabulary of shape; materials such as moulded plywood or the tubular steel of a bicycle's frame were employed to make strong, lightweight furniture. Improvements in construction and building materials had the potential to transform the home into a series of fluid light-filled spaces free from traditional constraints. Homes were 'machines for living' just as chairs were 'machines for sitting' in the pure logic of function.

Many of the classic designs in modern furniture date from this remarkable period of innovation and radicalism before the Second World War. But equally important, the period marked the emergence of a new way of conceiving interior space, an approach that remains as relevant today as it was sixty or seventy years ago. Houses in the nineteenth century were defined by a segregation of masters and servants, old and young, male and female, public and private, a hierarchical structure enshrined in the pattern of room use. In the radical designs of the 1920s and 1930s, houses were planned to accommodate activities or serve purposes; space was integrated, flexible, interconnected.

The modern spirit did not begin and end with the modernists of the 1920s and 1930s. Other important strands in contemporary

Above **Interior meets exterior, separated only by panes of glass in this Frank Lloyd Wright house. The skilful play of natural textures is characteristic of his work.**

Right **In this blue, white and grey bathroom, functionalism, in the form of hardwearing surfaces and exposed pipework, is beautifully complemented and enhanced by individual square glass panes, which provide several windows to the world.**

decorating date from the postwar era. The work of Scandinavian designers, such as Alvar Aalto and Arne Jacobsen, fused the clarity of modern forms with the humane and expressive qualities of materials such as wood and textiles to create a liveable, comfortable, modern look that fostered a new, informal lifestyle. The relaxed nature of such lifestyles was evident in the increasing popularity of the 'open plan' arrangement, a dissolution of traditional boundaries in the interior.

If the barriers came down inside the home, they also became practically invisible between indoors and out. Planes of glass — even, as in the case of Philip Johnson's Connecticut house built in 1949, entire walls of glass — extended living space into the world outside.

During the 1950s and 1960s new imagery, borrowed from science, the space age as well as pop, provided exciting themes for fabrics and furnishings, while new materials such as plastics brought an organic malleability to form. More recently, high-tech, although short-lived as a style, has had more of an enduring influence by blurring the distinctions between home and workplace. Utility fittings and furniture, from photographers' lights to warehouse system shelving, have migrated to the home, while the home itself may be fashioned from redundant factories, workshops and commercial premises. The airy expansive loft, with its raw industrial aesthetic, has brought a new sense of scale and drama to our ideas about interior space.

Although contemporary decorating may owe its origins to the pure visions of the first modernists, the relentless logic of functionalism has now been tempered by a keen awareness of the spiritual and sensual qualities that bring spaces alive and make them enjoyable, as well as practical. Shapes remain clean and defined, but they are just as likely to be curvy as rigidly rectilinear. In place of dogma, there is a new and welcome tolerance of the eclectic mix — not a stylistic free-for-all, but an acknowledgment of the importance of including the odd personal, idiosyncratic or even period piece.

Contemporary decorating is, if you like, 'new' modern — not the tautology it appears, but a reworking of modern design themes and a rediscovery of basic tenets.

Above **Bare does not necessarily mean cold. In this pared-down living area, natural light floods in through the undressed windows and ribbed plastic room dividers, while giant terracotta pots of box and weeping fig trees soften the space with texture and colour.**

GROUNDWORK

Decoration was a dirty word for early modern designers. 'Ornament is crime', was the severe judgement of Adolf Loos. In such a context, 'contemporary decorating' could be seen as a contradiction in terms: in the modern interior, so the argument goes, design is what matters; the rest is superfluous and unnecessary. But decoration need not imply stick-on style or redundant twiddly detail; it can be the expression, via colour, texture and material character, of elemental qualities that enhance our appreciation and enjoyment of space. The contemporary approach allows design and decoration to work in partnership.

It is easy enough for such a partnership to flow when the home is of relatively recent construction, or if it is flexible or anonymous in character and layout. Many apartments, for example, fall into this category. But contemporary decorating does not necessarily demand a modern framework to be successful. It is perfectly possible to create a contemporary scheme within a period house; in fact, the tension between an old structure and a modern style of decor can be very exciting. The fact that many lofts are the result of conversions of properties dating back well over a century is a case in point. But even domestic buildings with a past can house contemporary interiors.

In some cases, architects and designers have treated an older property merely as a shell and stripped back all internal partitions and levels to insert an entirely new interior within the volume of space. This capsule approach

may be the only way to gain a thoroughly modern home, in planning as well as decor, within a period house. But there are other less drastic strategies in keeping with most people's scope – and budget.

For contemporary decorating to work well in an older house, both sides of the equation must be treated with equal strength and respect. Contemporary decorating is emphatically not 'modernizing', that misguided attempt, so common in the 1960s, to bring Victorian and Edwardian rooms up to date by blocking off or removing all traces of the original architectural character without putting anything in their place. It is one thing to remodel entirely a house from the inside out, quite another to remove cornices, fireplaces and mouldings and leave a room denuded rather than transformed. By the same token, just because there is a Victorian fireplace in a room, it does not mean that the rest of the decor must necessarily and inevitably follow suit. Many period details work well in a robust juxtaposition with brilliant colour and sleek modern furnishings.

Contemporary decorating does entail at least some consideration of basic design matters: it is not enough simply to substitute a Corbusier chaise longue for the traditional sofa and hang a modern light fitting from the ceiling rose. Before decorating can begin, it is important to take a look at the fundamental disposition of space and the way the home is planned.

Older homes preserve the lifestyles of generations past. A Victorian terraced (row) house, for example, often has a separate dining room,

a living room on the main floor and a kitchen tucked away at the lower level. Nineteenth-century visitors may never have got much further than the parlour or sitting room, while the mistress of the household rarely strayed into the kitchen. Today, the segregation of activities implied by this arrangement is as undesirable as it is unworkable. We increasingly like to live, eat, entertain and even cook within the same space or series of connecting areas. Reorganizing the planning of a house so that the kitchen moves into a more central position or becomes absorbed within an open-plan living space brings the interior into line with our needs and desires. Equally, it is rare for a house from

Left Translucent pale blue cupboard doors alongside conventional white kitchen units inject colour into the room and prevent it from looking clinical and uninviting.

Below Underfloor heating is functional, decorative and luxurious, throwing warmth upwards into a room and freeing walls from space-filling radiators.

the previous century to offer much in the way of a visual link with the space that surrounds it. Improving connections with the outdoors can generate more natural light and a sense of openness and expansion.

Major structural alteration is outside the scope of this book, but it is worth bearing in mind that the best decorating results are achieved when the basic framework is right. At the simplest level, this can mean ensuring there are enough power points to sustain a lighting scheme, that natural light is maximized wherever possible, and that different areas in the home are designated and planned to serve the right functions.

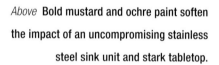

Above **Bold mustard and ochre paint soften the impact of an uncompromising stainless steel sink unit and stark tabletop.**

Above right **A cool blue splashback and a blue-tinted glass shelf give this bathroom an ethereal atmosphere. Accessories are hidden away in streamlined cupboards.**

CREATING A CONTEMPORARY SCHEME

The popular image of the modern interior consists of pure white walls, neutral flooring and a minimal arrangement of designer furniture. This is hardly surprising, since many modern architects and designers have replicated precisely this formula over the years, so much so that a particular kind of grey industrial-weight cord carpeting is almost a signature of the approach.

Contemporary decorating is by no means as reticent or predictable. Neutrality can be soothing, even challenging, but there is more to life than monochrome. Contemporary decorating has shed some of the more puritanical and worthy overtones of its origins and embraced the vibrant, evocative realm of the senses.

Colour is vital. Walls are blank canvases ready to be saturated in intense hues. There is nothing faint-hearted about the approach – no hints or insinuations of colour in muted pastel form. Searing, fashionable shades from all parts of the spectrum add verve and flair. Citrus greens and yellows, fruity tangerines, scorching fuchsias and deep moody blues provide stimulating backdrops to the crisp, clean lines of modern design. Even white is transformed, no longer the epitome of restraint, but layered white on white to make rooms of enveloping softness and luminous light.

Texture is another key to the look. As modern has matured, it has rediscovered the importance of texture as a means of providing depth and richness. Riveted metalwork, painted or exposed brickwork, frosted glass, silky

Left In this converted space, one brickwork wall is left unpainted for textural warmth, an effect echoed in the driftwood tables and wooden floor. The other walls, painted in neutral tones, and the off-white furnishings complete the natural look of the scheme.

smooth wood, offer a range of tactile experiences that add another dimension to living. The purely visual is not enough – different materials sound and feel different as we touch them, walk on them or sit on them, banishing the risk of dull uniformity.

In a related context, comfort has been brought back into the picture. Many people associate modern interiors with a lack of comfort, with ungiving hard surfaces and chairs that make 'statements' which are uncomfortable to sit in. While this may be true of the work of some modern designers, past and present, others specifically have addressed the need to accommodate the human frame in all its postures: even the master of modernism, Corbusier, designed a famous armchair called 'le Grand Confort'. But comfort has to be seen to be comfortable. Texture and softer materials such as textiles and rugs provide a domesticating layer that demonstrates the liveability of a room. Forms that curve and flow are easy on the eye. Comfort of a different order can be discovered in firelight and candlelight, in scent and flowers – evocative, spiritual details that soothe the soul.

Contemporary decorating also means thinking about scale. Modern living is all about ease and simplicity, about avoiding meaningless clutter and fussy detail. But if you reduce what a room contains, you must provide an anchor for what remains. One large sofa can do the trick for furniture arrangement; one large painting or picture for display; a large pattern can add drama to soft furnishing. By contrast, isolated objects or pieces of smaller proportions, dotted around a room, can make it look more like a modern gallery than a living space.

The quality of space is of fundamental importance. This does not necessarily mean you have to move walls around; the dynamics of space can be orchestrated with screens,

Right **Polished concrete has been used to great practical and aesthetic effect on this floor and dining table. Combined with areas of colour on white walls, and at the windows, a feeling of spaciousness is created.**

movable partitions and open dividers. New glazing in doors can draw light and views into the heart of the home. Clever fitted storage can make the between-spaces in halls and landings work harder to liberate the rooms you live in.

Bright, bold and positive, contemporary rooms are brimming with joie de vivre. Living in the moment has never been so much fun.

Above **Comfort and practicality are provided in the form of a squashy, inviting sofa and a mobile storage cabinet. With stairs leading to a galleried library, this is the contemporary equivalent of a period reading room.**

WALLS

WALLS

Walls define living space: they segregate activities, provide private enclaves and mark out separate domains within the home. They are also blank canvases, surfaces for creative expression. Both elements are key considerations for the contemporary decorator.

Walls have for some time been the focus of interest for those keen to demonstrate their decorative skills. The styles of the past have been ransacked like a dressing-up box, and a host of virtuoso techniques, from sponging to marbling, has been revived. But as walls have become busy with broken colour and pattern, and every available surface has been ragrolled to a standstill, there has been a renewed and belated appreciation of the importance of walls as background. When walls are so attention-seeking, rooms lack breathing space.

In the popular imagination, modern interiors equal plain white walls. Keeping walls uniformly white does give rooms a chance to breathe and it certainly relegates the walls to the background. Less than a century ago, such a treatment was startling and provocative, a stark contrast to the heavily patterned and highly coloured wallpapers of popular taste. Yet what was once radical and innovative can now seem merely bland and unadventurous. White has its place in the contemporary decorator's repertoire, but it needs to be treated positively, as a choice in its own right rather than as a decorating opt-out.

Between these two extremes – the stifling richness of the over-decorated wall and the nullity of the blank canvas – are a number of

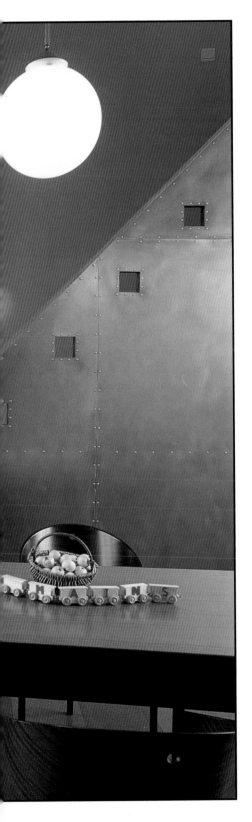

effective strategies that are able to generate both atmosphere and vitality without pushing walls too far into the foreground.

Concentrated planes of colour articulate space and create dynamic interest. Lightweight contemporary materials such as plywood, tile or metal sheeting can be used as wall cladding to bring added texture and depth of character. Raw plaster or bare brick can be exposed to give a rugged contrast to clean-lined furnishings, while open-plan areas can be partitioned with translucent glass brick or the sensuous curve of a wooden screen.

Left **Gloss paint applied to smooth walls has produced a pleasing sheen, which is echoed in this staircase of panelled aluminium. Rivets are driven into the metal to secure it to a wooden framework.**

Below **A kitchen area is half-concealed behind a bar-like divider lined with corrugated metal. Although the splashback is also of corrugated metal, the lines run horizontally, echoing the Venetian blind, which helps to increase the sense of space and give the kitchen its own identity.**

PAINT

Colour is a key element in contemporary decorating, and paint is one of the simplest ways of
providing our homes with this critical dimension. Unlike our ancestors, who could not get
enough of it, we tend to be rather more hesi-
tant about colour. Pre-industrialization, bright
colour was hard to achieve and consequently
expensive; those who could afford it, flaunted it
shamelessly. Paradoxically, colour today has
never been cheaper, easier or more reliable, but
many people fight shy of it altogether. This reluc-
tance is only exacerbated by the huge range of
paint colours available – a breadth of choice
that can be more bewildering than inspiring. But
as the worlds of fashion and interiors increasingly converge, there is a helping hand in colour

choice. There is no reason why our homes should not be as fashionable as our clothes, and with paint colour simple and inexpensive to change, we can enjoy surroundings that sing out with the colours of the moment.

The risk of such an approach is the possibility that we may tire of the wall colour rather more quickly than we are prepared to pick up a paintbrush and change it. But the fun of responding to the new can still be exciting and persuasive.

The palette for contemporary decorating is strong, bright and bold. When people think of strong colour, they often think in terms of paintbox primaries, the solid spectrum colours that enjoyed a brief vogue with high-tech. But strong colour today is sharper and more intense.

Above One-note colour schemes create an unbeatable sense of drama. The enveloping soft blue colour-wash on walls and ceiling, together with painted blue floor, generates a moody, restful atmosphere.

Left Fashion can be an exciting inspiration for home colour schemes. Cheap and easy to apply, paint is the perfect medium for instant makeovers.

Far left A wall of solid, earth red colour orchestrates space in a way that focuses the eye on both the black, graphic furniture and the vivid backdrop.

Above **Curvilinear walls are fascinating architectural elements for a large space. Painted a sharp terracotta, this wall creates a room within a room, bringing earthy colour relief to the natural landscape outdoors.**

in a bright colour while leaving the rest pure white. Alternatively, bright clashing colours, particularly from the same part of the spectrum such as scarlet, raspberry, salmon and coral, can look great in combination.

Matt textures let the colour speak for itself. Overtly distressed paint techniques are at odds with the contemporary look, but paint that has been rubbed or washed on the wall in dilute form can provide a translucent, shimmering effect to contrast with pristine floor finishes and fittings. For a slick finish, try painting walls in gloss – a great solution for kitchens and bathrooms where water-resistance is a priority. Gloss paint will show up lumps and bumps, however, and is best on near-perfect plasterwork.

Those in search of a quieter life can turn to more muted colours to provide a classic modern background. Again, fashion has been an inspiration, with the soft browns, taupes, mushrooms and beiges of camelhair, suede, leopardskin and tortoiseshell to the forefront. These sober, subtle shades, suggestive of different textures and materials, can be enlivened with sharp accents of burnt orange, pale blue and mint green, or dressed down with plenty of white to create a soothing, sensual atmosphere.

Finally, there is white. For the contemporary decorator only pure white will do. Off-white, magnolia, and any white with a hint of something else all run the risk of looking insipid, fainthearted and rather dull. Pure white, by contrast, lets in the light like no other shade.

White goes with anything, but what it goes with best is more white. An all-white scheme

Searing secondaries such as orange, violet, lime and fuchsia add vibrancy to the interior. Reds and blues that contain more than a hint of their opposite number have depth and potency. Defiantly artificial, such colours echo the brilliant shades of plastic and packaging rather than the discreet charm of the cottage garden. Darker and more mysterious are the innumerable shades of blue – everything from misty azure and fresh lavender to cobalt and indigo.

Strong colour needs a strong hand. Rather than paint all four walls the same shade, it can be more effective, and less tiring to live with, to treat walls as separate planes and pick out one makes spaces flow into each other or transforms a room into a private haven. Restful, clean and sharp, white is also luxurious. At the same time, it can be cruelly revealing. Imperfections of plasterwork will show up as readily as dirt, and clever lighting is essential to avoid the sterile, clinical look.

White on white has the minimalist's seal of approval, but it need not be stark. As a decorating strategy, it also has a respectable pedigree. One of the first to exploit the drama of white was Charles Rennie Mackintosh. The home he created with his wife Margaret Macdonald in turn-of-the-century Glasgow was shockingly avant-garde in its use of white – on walls, furniture and furnishings. The effect was soft, intimate and spiritual, an oasis of refinement in a grey industrial city. Later on in the twentieth century, society decorators such as Elsie de Wolfe and Syrie Maugham whitened walls and pickled wooden furniture to create the epitome of between-the-wars chic. These positive uses of white, as a way of focusing on texture and light, remain just as inspirational today.

Below **Monastic white walls and ceiling and minimal embellishment make this bedroom completely serene and allergy-free. Even everyday clutter is protected from dust in glass-fronted beech units that resemble traditional shopfitters' storage.**

PAPER

Wallpaper has been out of fashion for so long that cynics might say it is ripe for a come-back. In some circles, of course, it has never lost its popularity; chintzy and sprigged prints, Regency stripes and stately classical patterns all have their loyal fans. This loose family of period-style designs seems to sum up all that is contrary to the contemporary spirit in design.

But in many previous periods when modernity was much closer to mainstream taste, wallpapers were produced that fitted in perfectly with the prevailing progressive mood. Classic patterns included geometric machine-age motifs from the 1930s, organic designs inspired by discoveries in science and technology from the 1950s, pop designs from the 1960s and shiny disco-style papers from the 1970s. Just as fabric patterns can reflect contemporary themes, such designs proved that papering a wall need not be intrinsically reactionary.

Wallpaper remains popular because it is a practical way of hiding surface imperfections. If you live in an older home and have gone to the trouble of stripping off layers of paper to reveal the bare plaster underneath, you are unlikely to be left with a pristine surface.

Right **This inventive, streamlined staircase with wooden cladding is carefully designed to provide a graphic counterpoint to the steel grey painted wall, which includes an integral unit for the television and pull-out drawers, and the adjacent brick wall.**

In some circumstances, battered plaster may not be too much of an eyesore, but if it is and you cannot afford to replaster, wallpaper hides a multitude of sins.

In the mass market, wallpaper designs with contemporary appeal are thin on the ground. Look out for bold geometrics or very narrow stripes; some hand-printed papers have a distinctly Art Deco feel. Alternatively, if the search proves too frustrating, you can make your own. Print simple designs on to lining paper using wood blocks, stamps or linocuts; blow up intriguing found images Fornasetti-style on the photocopier; paste up wrapping paper or maps – use whatever is strong and graphic and displays the colours you like.

CLADDING

The character of raw materials is another element that can be explored in the context of contemporary wall decoration. Wall cladding makes practical sense in many situations: putting up a robust or washable surface behind stoves, sinks and around the bath is always a good idea. But panels of different materials can have aesthetic impact, too, giving walls a material dimension that invites touch and reflects light in different and intriguing ways.

Wood is the classic cladding material. Plain pine cladding, readily available in tongued-and-grooved boards, can be painted or left natural with the merest coat of matt varnish to seal the timber. Plywood also looks impressive on walls.

Left **A bare expanse of biscuit-coloured wallpaper provides a neutral background for a display of typed sheets of poetry.**

Above **Elegant cladding is both headboard and decoration in this white, textural bedroom. Square panels of hardwood have been laid so that the grains mismatch, to produce varied wood tones. A thin lip of darker wood forms the edging.**

walls for a gleaming, reflective surface. Rubbing down with wire wool and subsequent waxing will give a burnish to the metal. (Bear in mind that if you apply sheet metal around or near power points, you will need the help of an electrician to earth this very conductive material.)

For transparent panels that reveal the underlying wall colour, try wired security glass, corrugated plastic or Perspex (Plexiglas). Large steel mesh panels fixed to the wall can be the perfect solution for suspending kitchen utensils from hooks, while a large sheet of mirror glass will multiply views and vistas for an increased sense of space.

Tiling is a tried-and-tested formula for areas of heavy wear or maximum exposure to water and heat. Adopt a whole-hearted approach and tile the entire wall, not just the area next to the sink, bath or stove – small tiled panels look skimpy and ill-considered.

Tiling provides the opportunity to play with scale as well as colour. The tiny grid of mosaic makes a good-looking modern surface, especially in a strong single colour or in a random abstract arrangement where individual tiles of contrasting shades or gold, mirror or glass are set against the main field of colour. Sheets of mosaic are available ready-made in such random designs, making installation simple. Mosaic is particularly effective in bathrooms: the small scale of the grid suits the restrictions of area and the softness of the effect belies the practicalities of this hard, resistant surface. Mirror mosaic, also available in sheets, will make a crisp, glittery border.

Large panels can be screwed in place and trimmed with flat moulding to make a gridded effect. Flush plywood sheets or thin wood veneer at the head of a bed will create a warm sense of enclosure for a sleeping space.

For smaller areas, particularly splashbacks and bathroom surfaces, investigate materials that have a tough, industrial edge. Pliable zinc sheeting can be nailed, stuck or screwed on to

Left Deep turquoise mosaic tiles appear to envelop the bath, creating a tranquil retreat while protecting the walls from water – appealing as well as practical.

Below The skilful placing of zinc, wood and porcelain in this bathroom shows how important materials are in establishing the right atmosphere.

Reminiscent of grand hotel bathrooms between the wars, rectangular or metro-style tiling has a particularly contemporary appeal. Even more luxurious (and expensive) are luminous hand-glazed ceramic tiles that bring the charm of irregularity to what is essentially a machine-made product.

If you have inherited tiling in a colour you hate, cover up the offending shade with paint. The tiles must be perfectly clean and dry before you begin. Then apply a base coat and two top coats of oil-based paint in the colour you prefer for an instant revamp.

Below **A uniform application of white tiles is an enduring solution for bathrooms that incorporate baths and showers. The effect is clean and restful; the addition of brightly coloured towels and accessories will soften the space and prevent a clinical feel.**

STRIPPING

You can also introduce material interest by stripping off existing finishes or leaving walls in what might otherwise be considered an 'unfinished' state. In older homes and industrial buildings, some walls may consist of solid blockwork. Areas of brickwork or stone walling can be sandblasted and sealed to expose the character and texture of the raw material.

Unpainted or uncovered plaster is another surface rich with associations. Plaster comes in a range of colours, from a pinkish beige reminiscent of fresco to a greyish industrial white. Leaving plaster more or less untreated is a

strong modern look in itself. Notionally 'honest', although in reality a decorative choice like any other, exposed plaster is easy to enjoy for its soft, matt texture. The warmer tones look particularly good in contrast with gleaming metal furnishings and fittings, while off-white plaster can be mixed with kaolin to give a chalky porcelain finish that is also extremely attractive and subtly different from a plastered wall that has been painted white. Bare plaster has a tendency to 'dust', so some form of seal is desirable. A thin coat of wax or seal may darken the plaster; adding a little white paint to the seal will help to counteract this effect.

Above left **Some walls need no embellishment to make a strong decorative statement. This original, indigenous stone is colour enough, counterbalanced with wood and metal elsewhere in the room.**

Above **Raw concrete has been treated with a colourwash of steely grey, making a soft, textured backdrop for a marble-floored entrance hall where natural light illuminates and orchestrates the space.**

DETAIL

Decorating walls is not merely a question of surface treatment. Architectural detail, such as skirting boards and cornices, can also be an important factor, despite the relatively small amount of surface area they occupy. In older houses, such features are likely to be more ornate and overt and the success of a contemporary scheme can depend to some extent on how these elements are treated.

In the recent past, many original architectural details, from cornices to ceiling roses, were removed in the somewhat misguided spirit of modernization. Today, we rightly regard such a strategy as no less than vandalism and have learned to respect what evidence remains of a building's heritage. Many rooms that once were stripped of mouldings, decorative plasterwork and even fireplaces have since seen these features painstakingly reinstated, either in the form of salvaged parts or in reproduction. All too often, decoration has then followed suit, with respect for original features translated into slavish subservience to period detail.

But just as the presence of Victorian cornicing does not mean you have to turn the clock back to 1880, contemporary decorating does not mean you have to eradicate every last feature older than yesterday. Painting mouldings, cornicing and skirting (baseboards) in with the main wall colour can lessen their prominence as heritage-markers while leaving an interior's architectural past intact. Similarly, painting woodwork a strong contrasting or complementary colour can also be very effective.

Above **A classic fireplace, stripped back to the essentials of brick recess and marble hearth bordered in wood, is a surprisingly modern element in a traditional room, proving that contemporary need not mean harsh and uninviting.**

Many of these details also serve at least some practical function. Skirtings protect the base of the wall from damage. Cornicing disguises the superficial cracking that occurs where planes of plasterwork meet. Picture rails, of course, speak for themselves, and if you retain such features today, it is important to use them for their intended purpose.

In modern houses, there is the opportunity to reduce detailing. Minimalists attempt to do without such features altogether, eschewing all architraves, mouldings and even skirtings. Walls can be stopped fractionally short on inset beading, so they appear to hover over the floor; window and door openings left bare of any surrounding framework. The cost of such a strategy can, however, be high. Doing without mouldings entirely tends to mean that plasterwork has to be uniformly smooth, with razor-sharp edges and true right-angles, a degree of perfection that can be difficult and expensive to achieve.

For a modernist detail, try metal skirtings – but consult an electrician to make sure the metal is earthed! Plain ply skirting can also be very effective, especially when it is combined with metal socket plates.

Left **This daring transformation from period home to chic living space is hugely successful, combining traditional architectural features, such as cornices and a spiral staircase, with pared-down walls, integral storage and modern furnishings.**

Above This floor of a period town house has been completely opened up to provide a living space at one end and a kitchen/dining area at the other. A dividing wall has been created by a refrigerator and kitchen units.

Right One-room living is made more elegant with a subtle screen of ribbed plastic that glides gently along a wooden floor, blurring the view from the eating area to the sleeping area but without blocking the light.

DIVIDING SPACE

The open plan is a classically modern way of arranging space. Multi-purpose areas that serve complementary functions, such as living and eating, eating and cooking, have become increasingly more popular than the traditional method of apportioning space in self-contained and separate rooms. Like many contemporary ideas, the concept is not new. As one writer has pointed out, the generously proportioned kitchen/living room of modern times is somewhat akin to the old medieval hall. This way of using space means that internal or partition

walls are often redundant. Knocking two rooms together by removing the wall that separates them is one of the commonest forms of structural alteration (see also Windows & Doors, pages 73–4).

Houses opened up from back to front and top to bottom to make soaring, double-height, open-plan spaces may be dramatic, but without a degree of care they can be unliveable. Some distinction between activities will always be necessary for practical reasons, such as privacy and soundproofing. Aesthetically, too, a large expanse can be oddly featureless and inhuman in scale without a few boundaries to break up the space.

The answer is not necessarily to revert to the old pattern of separate rooms for separate purposes. Screens, transparent partitions and half-height barriers can serve to orchestrate space, direct traffic flows and provide some sense of enclosure without the need to create the full stop of a permanent, solid boundary.

Left **Glass bricks appear to denote the end of a space but in fact screen off a kitchen. Two additional rooms have been created with movable walls of sliding wooden panels painted a turquoise blue.**

On the simplest and most straightforward level, space can be divided by free-standing screens. Many contemporary designers have produced elegant modern versions in sinuous curving plywood or intriguingly articulated panels. Free-standing open dividers in wood, metal or metal and glass can also serve the same function. For a slightly more permanent feature, you can fit an opening with the type of sliding or top-hung, concertina screen that is often used to partition school rooms. This would be an ideal solution for a large children's room, turning a shared playroom into two separate bedrooms at night. Window-like Japanese *shoji* screens, with their rice-paper 'glazing' and black lacquered mullions, create a sense of calm and soften the light. You can vary the style by using beech or other blond wood for the framing and Tyvek for the glazing; this is a new paper-like material that incorporates polyethylene fibres.

For permanent room dividers that also let in light, glass brick is the perfect solution. Invented in Germany before the First World War, it was a favoured building material of early modernists. Like other modernist preferences such as plywood and concrete, glass brick also remained overlooked until relatively recently, tainted with a utilitarian image that arose from its widespread industrial use. Today, it has been rediscovered with a vengeance.

Glass brick combines the structural strength and properties of brick or blockwork with the translucency of glass. It lets in light, but at the same time obscures views, so privacy

Below **In this open-plan kitchen and dining area, the busy cooking zone is screened from view with a panel of glass bricks, which enhance the decor without encroaching on the working space.**

can be maintained. It provides acoustic insulation and, unlike plate glass, does not result in unwanted heat loss or gain.

For dividing space without sacrificing a sense of spaciousness, glass brick is ideal. As a staircase enclosure, as a large half-width partitioning panel, as a wall separating an internal bathroom, shower or kitchen from the rest of the living space, glass brick blocks most of the views, all of the sound and none of the light. In terraced (row) houses, with windows only at front and rear, drawing light into central spaces is a priority. Glass brick partitions mean that internal rooms can borrow light from areas that are directly lit. Like all such treatments, it works best as a whole-hearted solution, not as small decorative panels.

Left Glass bricks are particularly valuable in rooms where there is little natural light. Here, a small screen provides privacy and allows light from the upper floor to filter through.

Below Walls that divide and screen are versatile additions to spaces that have two or more functions. This wall both supports washbasins and acts as a headboard.

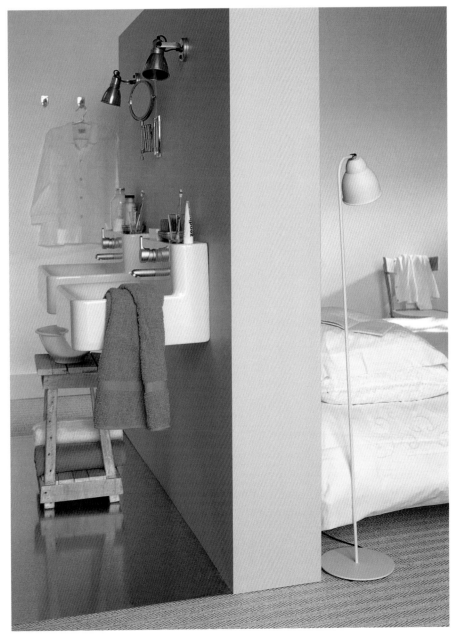

The bricks come in a variety of sizes, colours and finishes, from clear to sandblasted and patterned. They are relatively expensive and should be laid professionally because of their weight and the binding agents used. In certain situations, steel rods need to be incorporated between the courses for fire separation, and it is important to check that your new construction complies with local building regulations.

If you do not wish to lose a wall entirely, but need to open up internal views, you can create indoor windows to connect areas visually. Portholes are very graphic and a good means of introducing light into internal kitchens or bathrooms. Similarly, if you need to install a partition wall, a gently curving shape can introduce a more dynamic effect than a straight plane.

Dividing screen

This scrupulously simple, semi-opaque screen provides a discreet space divider at the top of a flight of stairs. As well as delineating the start of the room, it also allows some natural light through to the staircase. Fitted to floor and ceiling on aluminium tracking, the ribbed plastic easily slots into position.

The same device could be used to great effect elsewhere in the home where space needs to be punctuated but not completely interrupted, such as in a kitchen/diner where you might want to separate the cooking area from the dining table. It could also be applied to cupboard doors on wall-mounted storage units in a kitchen or living room, where the ribbed plastic disguises the contents without screening them off completely.

Both the tracking and ribbed plastic can be bought at hardware stores. The plastic is available in different thicknesses and therefore degrees of opacity. For our screen, we used 2cm (¾in) thick plastic.

MATERIALS AND TOOLS

• Metal tape measure • Ribbed plastic, cut to fit • 2 sections of aluminium tracking, cut to fit • Piece of scrap wood or workbench • Power drill, drill bit and countersink bit • Screwdriver • Countersunk screws

METHOD

Measure the area for the screen and order up a piece of ribbed plastic to fit. If it needs further cutting, a tenon saw (backsaw) should suffice.

1 Place one section of aluminium tracking on a piece of scrap wood on the floor, so that the floor is protected when you drill, or on a workbench. With the power drill make holes at 15cm (6in) intervals along the floor tracking. Do the same for the ceiling tracking. (Alternatively, you can use pre-drilled tracking.)

2 Cut a recess in the track for the screw heads with a countersink bit (the screw heads must be flush with the track so that the screen slides smoothly into the mountings). Screw the tracking to the floor and ceiling with counter-sunk screws. Slide in the screen to fit.

Colourful canvases

These wall hangings give new meaning to the expression 'blank canvas'. Painted whatever shade you desire, they are an excellent means of creating your own colour statement in a room. You can also vary the size and shape to suit your decor.

We fixed our canvases to the wall very simply: with nails. For heavier canvases, which may need more support, you can make two holes in the frame, thread through thick chandler's rope and then knot it at both ends. The rope needs to be pulled as tightly as possible across the back of the canvas so that there is no slack and the canvas is held as closely as possible to the wall. The rope is then hooked over a strong metal bracket that has been driven into the wall.

MATERIALS AND TOOLS

• Pre-stretched and primed artists' canvases
• Matt emulsion paint • Paint kettle • 10cm (4in) paintbrush • Hammer and masonry nails
• Straightedge • Spirit level • Pencil

METHOD

While we used pre-stretched canvases, which are available from any good artists' suppliers, you may want to stretch your own. To do this, you will need a frame, or stretcher, also available from an artists' suppliers. Stretch your piece of canvas tightly over the frame and secure with a staple gun.

Make sure you have enough paint for two coats. This is particularly important if the colours you have chosen are strong.

1 The frame of the bottom canvas hangs from two nails hammered into the wall, one at either end of the top edge of the canvas. Decide on the position of the bottom canvas and hammer in the left-hand nail accordingly.

2 With the straightedge pushed against the left-hand nail and using the spirit level, locate the position for the right-hand nail. Mark with a pencil. Hammer in the nail. Hang the frame from the two nails.

The simplest way to hang the two smaller canvases above the larger one is to rest them on top of the bottom canvas. Hammer in two nails just above each of the top canvases to make sure they rest neatly on top of the bottom canvas and are securely in place. The nails at

the top will not be noticed in a room where the seating is at a lower level than the canvases.

3 A completely different look can be created by separating and moving the canvases.

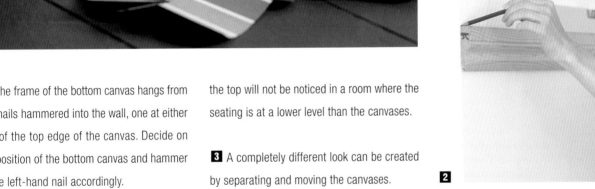

Painted target

The red, white and blue target was a powerful 1960s pop-culture icon. Here it is softened with colour to make a truly contemporary statement on a living room wall.

Flat colour on a wall can be jazzed up by applying matt and gloss paints side by side. Gloss paint has been in the doldrums for a couple of decades because of its toxicity, but it is making a dramatic comeback as a new generation of designers experiment with it in its more eco-friendly form.

This technique can be applied to many different motifs, grids or loose patterns. Vertical stripes lend formality, doing away with the need for strait-laced wallpaper; four large squares can echo colourful wall hangings or pictures; or glossy spots painted randomly or in lines can

provide space-age chic. The smartest effects come from using matt and gloss paints in identical colours, but you can also vary the colours of both paints for pop-art opulence.

MATERIALS AND TOOLS

• 10cm (4in) paintbrush or 30cm (12in) roller
• 5cm (2in) paintbrush • Matt emulsion paint
• Gloss paint in the same colour • String
• Pencil • Steel rule • Block of wood • Hand drill • Drawing pin or tack

METHOD

Prepare the wall by washing. If the wall is uneven, sand and fill to a smooth surface. Apply a coat of emulsion paint with the 10cm (4in) brush or roller. (Brushes usually produce a

smoother surface.) You may need to apply a second coat if you have chosen a deep colour. Leave to dry. Find the centre of the proposed target by pinning two lengths of string diagonally from each corner of the wall area you want to decorate. Make a pencil mark at the centre and remove the string.

1 With the steel rule, measure out from the centre of the target and mark the diameter of the first circle. (Our circles are spaced roughly 45cm/18in apart from one another.) Take the block of wood and drill a hole just big enough to house the pencil snugly. Tie one end of the piece of string to a drawing pin or tack and push in the drawing pin at the centre point. Tie the other end of the string around the wood. Push the pencil through the hole in the wood so that it protrudes through the other side. The distance from the drawing pin to the pencil should equal the radius of the circle. Using the block of wood like a compass, and keeping the pencil at right angles to the wall, trace the circumference of the first circle around the centre mark. Ours is about 45cm (18in) across. Repeat the process for the two outer circles, making sure the distance between them is the same.

2 Take the smaller brush and load it with gloss paint (be sure not to overload it as it will drip). Carefully paint the centre circle and the outer band with gentle brush strokes. To paint a smooth edge to the circles, push the brush up to within millimetres of the pencil lines. Leave to dry. Apply a second coat if necessary.

1

2

FLOORS

The floor sets the tone of the interior, intruding on our consciousness in all manner of ways beyond the visual. The way a floor sounds when you walk across it, or feels when you lounge on it, can be as crucial as its appearance. It is a background you simply cannot afford to ignore.

Flooring provides the opportunity to exploit the vital dimension of texture, to experiment with unusual materials and to enhance the sense of spaciousness. Because of the impact it will have, in both a practical and aesthetic sense, there is a very sound argument for choosing your flooring before you embark on anything else. New flooring can be expensive, and even reclaiming or refinishing old floors demands a great deal of time and effort. But, it must be said, no other aspect of the interior will repay the investment so richly.

Contemporary decorators have an enormous range of materials, colours and patterns from which to choose. And a host of materials that are not traditionally associated with flooring have come to the forefront, such as glass, metal and even leather. There really is no need to play safe and stay with what you know, and every reason to go for the unexpected.

For generating a sense of expansiveness, the harder flooring materials have the edge. From the chic brutality of polished concrete to the sophistication of wood strip, a hard floor makes a clean sweep of the interior, creating a bold, uncluttered base that gives a fundamental strength to the rest of the decor. Such materials have an almost structural quality that suits the no-frills modern aesthetic.

Softer materials that are more readily replaced, such as carpet and linoleum, have their own appeal. They are generally cheaper, easier to maintain and more comfortable underfoot than hard floors. They are also popular, but this does mean that you have to work just a little bit harder to avoid the obvious solution. But your soft floor need not be conventional in appearance; funky colours and patterns, as well as utility or 'industrial' materials, introduce freshness and vigour.

The contemporary interior does not necessarily require new flooring. Old or existing floors, particularly those made of plain wooden boards, parquet, stone or any other material that has a basic integrity, provide a perfect complement. Time-worn and characterful, such floors throw sleek modern fittings and decor into sharp relief: a robust contrast of styles can be extremely effective at anchoring a contemporary decorating scheme within the context of a much older setting.

Left **The mellow tones of renovated hardwood parquet make a soothing complement to simple contemporary furnishings and light, pure decoration.**

Far left **The metal treadplate and sturdy scaffolding poles give this stairway an industrial edge. The main kitchen flooring consists of square steel sheets.**

WOOD

Clean-lined but not punishingly hard, warm but not overly intimate, wood is deservedly one of the most popular of all flooring materials. A wooden floor works in almost any situation, both practically and aesthetically, and is available in a wide variety of formats for every budget and taste. It lasts well, ages beautifully and provides the perfect base for decorative rugs. The pattern of boards, blocks or strips in which it is laid prevents even large expanses of wood from looking monotonous.

The undisputed classic contemporary floor is hardwood strip. Ash, beech, maple and oak are the species most commonly used: each has its own characteristic grain, texture and colour, but the natural tones can be altered by staining, bleaching or varnishing. Paler finishes have a cool, pristine sophistication that works well in a contemporary setting.

The most durable and expensive version is solid strip. It comes in a variety of thicknesses, lengths and widths – thicker, wider and longer boards being the most costly. But this larger format is also the freshest-looking; narrow strip flooring is almost a victim of its own success and can sometimes be more suggestive of an upmarket retail outlet or gallery space than a home.

Rather more evocative is the variety of wood strip flooring that incorporates coloured neoprene between the boards. The rubber, which takes up any movement caused by variations in temperature or humidity, also reduces slipperiness, a vital function in its original use as ship's decking.

Most types of strip flooring are supplied tongue-and-grooved so that planks fit together without leaving any gaps. Provided the tongue is far enough below the surface, strip flooring can be refinished by sanding when the surface has worn unacceptably. This increases the life of the floor and prolongs your investment.

More affordable are 'manufactured' versions of strip flooring, consisting of a veneer of hardwood over a softwood or composition wood base, which is sometimes backed with cork. These floors are comfortable, resilient and relatively easy to install but they cannot be refinished. Many even come pre-sealed – there is no need to varnish or wax them.

Right **Industrial chic in the form of a steel and glass staircase is tempered with a wood floor. Its soft and warm appearance is a welcome contrast to the hard surfaces found elsewhere in this airy top-floor room.**

The way in which a floor is laid contributes a great deal to the dynamics of space. Strips that are laid lengthways down a room lead the eye onwards; laid diagonally, the effect will be of greater movement and vitality. Shorter strips of flooring can be laid in herringbone fashion, like traditional parquet.

Reclaiming or restoring an original wooden floor is one of the most economical shortcuts to contemporary style. Stripped floorboards are the signature of 'back to basics' simplicity – natural, neutral and easy on the eye.

Above left **The pale tones of an ash floor, table and chairs extend still further the feeling of light and space in this dining room. Window frames in a darker wood bring definition to the scheme.**

Left **Thin strips of beech flooring continue from the landing to the stairs on this pleasingly curved stairwell. The simple chrome stair rails, which follow the architectural curves, are an apposite contrast.**

In older homes, such as Victorian and Edwardian terraces (row houses), floorboards can usually be found at every level, laid horizontally across the room, resting on the joists that run from the front of the house to the back. In newer homes, ground-level flooring is likely to be concrete, but the floors on upper levels are usually boarded. The wood in both cases is generally pine. Older apartments and lofts converted from warehouses or schools may have original hardwood parquet, strip or block. The basic renovation procedure is more or less the same.

In nearly all instances, sanding will be necessary, to strip off old finishes and provide a level, smooth floor. You may have to undertake a number of repairs before sanding, such as replacing missing, rotten or damp boards (and correcting the problem that has caused the damp in the first place), filling gaps, securing loose boards, sinking nailheads and cleaning off old polish, wax or paint.

Sanding itself is arduous, dirty and potentially dangerous. Equipment can be rented cheaply, but you must be confident of your skills and strong enough to carry out the work effectively. If you employ a professional to do the job for you, the expense should still be much less than the cost of a new floor covering.

Sanded boards and hardwood floors need several coats of wax, sealant or varnish to prevent water and dirt from penetrating the grain and wearing away at the wood. The

Below **The joys of open-plan living include having a floor that requires minimal care and maintenance. This floor has been restored with reclaimed timber, sanded and polished to a waxy sheen.**

Above **A beautiful fusion of browns, taupes and different textures creates an air of relaxed calm in a room where a painted canvas provided the inspiration for the colour scheme. The timber floor, with its mellow tones, extends the colour as well as enriching the texture.**

problem with sealing pine floorboards is that it often results in a rather harsh and orange appearance. To prevent this, you can bleach the boards first to lighten the tone. A proprietary lightener or wood bleach will take out almost all the colour and give the finished floor the same look of cool sophistication normally achieved with a pricier hardwood. Alternatively, you can lime the boards by rubbing white paint, liming wax or gesso into the grain of the wood.

Bare sanded boards also make a perfect surface for colour. Wood stains, which come in a wide range of shades as well as wood tones, sink into the wood and leave the grain visible. For opaque coverage, apply paint. The boards will need a couple of coats of undercoat; then for the final finish you can choose between shiny gloss paint, matt eggshell, hard-wearing floor paint or exceptionally tough yacht or deck paint. The harder-wearing paints are expensive, more difficult to apply and take longer to dry. Eggshell will need a matt seal for protection, but all the other types of paint require no further sealing.

If you love wood but cannot afford new hardwood flooring and your floorboards are too battered to salvage, plywood provides a stylish and economical alternative. Manufactured from thin sheets of wood glued together, plywood is strong, flexible and attractively utilitarian. Flooring plywood is generally birch- or maple-faced, or birch throughout, and is available in sheets or squares, and tongued-and-grooved for easy laying. It can be stained or painted, or simply sealed with lacquer to bring out its warm, golden tones.

STONE

From creamy limestone to dark blue slate, stone brings a depth of richness and character to the interior. For such a traditional material, and one with many cultural and historic overtones, it can be surprisingly contemporary. Cool, graphic and hard-edged, stone floors provide an understated sense of luxury in modern rooms. In hot climates, stone makes a sophisticated floor throughout the home; where the weather is less kindly, it adds drama and distinction to hallways, kitchens and bathrooms.

Stone is incredibly varied, in colour, pattern, texture and format. The thicker, larger flags or tiles are extremely expensive. They must be laid professionally, and require a solid subfloor to bear their great weight.

Right **Blue-grey slate tiles blend well with beech kitchen cabinets and stainless steel surfaces. Slate and wood make a classic partnership of sleek modernity.**

Below **Floors can divide rooms and spaces as successfully as walls. Here, a hardwood strip floor merges into large limestone flags, separated by a thin dividing line.**

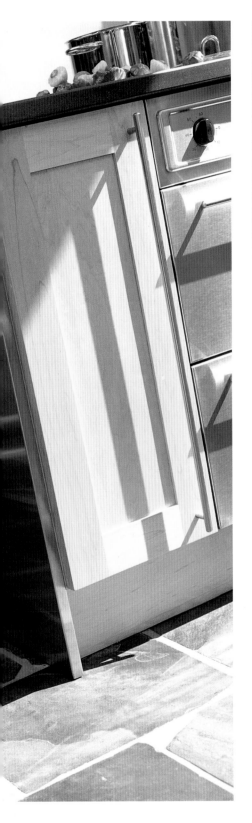

In a modern context, limestone makes a supremely elegant choice. It comes in a range of colours and textures, but the pale neutral tones are most successful in a contemporary scheme. The surface may be faintly patterned and textured, sometimes revealing the fossilized remains of marine creatures. Large, evenly sized flags have an architectural quality.

Slate is a good choice for an evocative modern floor. Colour is a strong selling point, with moody dark blues, greys and grey-greens being typical. The surface of the stone can be rippled or polished smooth.

Above **Weathered stone slabs connect the exterior to this generous hallway, their rippled texture providing a comfortable surface underfoot. Although a traditional flooring material, stone can look particularly chic in settings such as this.**

HARD TILES

Cheaper than stone and easier to handle and lay, hard tiles have a crisp, regular appearance that provides the perfect complement to clean, modern lines. In a contemporary setting, ceramic tiles are the best choice, as they do not share the more rustic connotations of terra-cotta or quarry tiles.

Because they are machine-made, ceramic tiles are precise and regular in dimension and colouring. The larger sizes make a classic gridded pattern, which is soothing and serene; smaller tiles look busier and are best suited to more restricted floor areas. Colour and texture vary incredibly, from discreet neutrals to bright primaries; some varieties are non-slip.

Above right **A dark wood strip floor butts up to biscuit-coloured tiling, the strong colour contrast indicating a change of function in this open-plan living space.**

Right **White ceramic floor tiles extend up the walls and reflect a pleasing dance of watery light as the sun streams through the glass brick wall. Ceramic tiles work particularly well in bathrooms, where their toughness and practicality are appreciated.**

Left To make this small kitchen appear larger, it was decorated white. As a white floor would have been inappropriate, black, white and grey mosaic tiles were laid to echo the cool grey of the stainless steel worktops – a decorative and practical solution.

Below Mosaic tiles in a uniform colour are the perfect flooring material where a variety of colours and surfaces meet. They can be laid in sheet form rather than painstakingly applied in single lines.

MOSAIC

The small scale of the grid gives mosaic an almost soft appearance. Tiny cubes of stone, terracotta, marble or ceramic bedded in mortar make a luminous floor vibrant with colour. Because the technique is labour-intensive and, consequently, rather expensive, mosaic is best restricted to small areas such as bathrooms.

Mosaic has often been the vehicle for pictorial designs but, in a modern interior, striking effects can be achieved with geometric patterning or a more random distribution of colour.

Above This concrete floor has been painted a deep blue with specialist concrete gloss paint. Tough polyurethane varnish will render the floor even shinier as well as protecting the surface from scratches and scuffs.

Far right Machine-pressed steel flooring is high-tech, high style and purely industrial, but it suits small areas, such as this compact kitchen, extremely well. Its hard surface complements the brushed iron splashback and contrasts pleasingly with the wood floor in the dining area.

Right Terrazzo flooring never fails to make a strong decorative statement. Here, it forms the basis of a monochromatic colour scheme in a light-filled and relaxing living space. It has also been used in slabs for the treads on a contemporary, concrete, spiral staircase.

CONCRETE

The quintessential modern material, concrete provokes extreme reactions. Brutal, raw and defiantly undecorative, it seems to encapsulate everything we most love to hate about modern building. Yet after years of being shunned for its soulless utility, rehabilitation is well underway.

It may seem inconceivable that this basic, monumental material, most commonly associated with multi-storey car parks, should have a

can be added to the basic mix; alternatively, it can be painted with special floor paint. For the sleekest and most sophisticated effect of all, concrete can be covered with acrylic or epoxy resin toppings. The finish is exceptionally glossy and looks almost liquid.

TERRAZZO

Terrazzo is a relative newcomer to the domestic scene, being a material more commonly seen in commercial interiors. Like other such crossovers, however, the associations with hotels, restaurants and other public places heighten its appeal. Terrazzo is an aggregate of marble or granite chippings mixed with cement and either laid in situ or as slabs or tiles. Either format is expensive and requires professional installation. Sleek, lively and subtly colourful, terrazzo makes a stylish floor in entrances and bathrooms, as well as living areas in hot climates.

METAL

Metal flooring provides another opportunity to experience the shock of the new. Aluminium or galvanized steel sheets are normally textured with a relief pattern, in designs such as tread-plate, to make a non-slip surface. In small doses, the much softer zinc can also be used on the floor, but it is very slippery and scratches quite easily. For enthusiastic modernists, the associations of metal flooring with industrial-style utility, ocean liners and aircraft are irresistible. Metal flooring can be laid over any level surface, timber or concrete, and may be either glued or screwed in place.

GLASS

Contemporary decor celebrates transparency in all forms, and the see-through floor is a logical extension of the approach. Glass flooring on mezzanine levels and staircases is supremely theatrical. Each floor must be individually specified and constructed by a specialist from thick annealed float glass, with sandblasted friction bars to stop the surface being excessively slippery.

Above **An ingenious mix of sandblasted glass and wood flooring has a striped, rug-like effect against a metal mesh staircase.**

domestic application, but as a final floor concrete has much to recommend it. Few surfaces are as hard, cold and ungiving, yet paradoxically, can look as soft and matt as suede. As a setting for strong modern furniture in chrome and leather, concrete has unbeatable machismo.

Concrete can also be treated in a variety of ways to alter its texture and colour. Patterns can be created by scoring or by embedding stones in the floor while it is still wet, and the final floor sealed and polished. To add colour but preserve the soft-looking texture, pigments

Right **Once the signature flooring of high-tech design, rubber stud flooring is enjoying a revival, its glossy surface and relative warmth appreciated by a new generation.**

Below **Vinyl is still a popular and economical choice for kitchen flooring. Used in classic chequerboard designs or as solid colour, it is unobtrusive but practical, and, in the right setting, utterly contemporary.**

LEATHER

The ultimate in bespoke flooring, leather spells the height of luxury and indulgence – a sensualist's dream. While it is a dream with a price tag, leather is perhaps more practical and durable than you might first imagine.

Flooring leather comes in tiles made from tough steer hide, dyed in a range of warm natural colours from reds and browns to dark green and black. Like leather upholstery it is not immune to scratches, but signs of wear are part of its character. Leather is not water-resistant and so is unsuitable for kitchens and bathrooms, but should withstand minor spills, if well waxed. It can be laid over a level hardboard or plywood base and bonded in place with contact adhesive.

LINOLEUM

Available in sheet or tile form and in a quite comprehensive range of colours and patterns, lino is enjoying a newfound surge of popularity, particularly among the style-conscious and the environmentally aware.

After decades of eclipse, its rediscovery has been prompted by improvements in practical performance and looks, backed up by impeccable natural credentials. Prewar lino was often a dreary, brittle, lurid material; in contrast, the modern product is strong, durable and exceptionally stylish. Composed entirely of natural ingredients, such as linseed oil, pine resin, cork and wood flour, it is anti-static, anti-bacterial, comfortable, warm, quiet and resilient – almost everything you could ever want from a flooring material.

Once restricted to hallways and corridors, kitchens, bathrooms and utility areas, lino is now ready to take centre stage. Sheet linoleum provides a seamless, integrated covering; tiles are easier for amateurs to install. Sheet lino can be cut and pieced in bold designs that demarcate space within an open-plan area; computer-controlled cutting also makes possible very intricate inlaid patterns for a custom design. Sheet lino is also available in geometric patterns, such as over-scaled gingham checks and plaids, though marbled, mottled or streaked finishes are standard. Colour choice is very broad, but even the more intense shades have a natural, soft look.

black and grey are still available, along with the searing primaries more typical of high-tech, but new, softer secondary colours as well as marbled and flecked patterns have vastly extended the decorative potential.

Rubber flooring is available in sheet or tile, with a smooth finish or in relief. Studded, ribbed, or treadplate surfaces counteract its basic disadvantage: its slipperiness. Like many ideas lifted from their industrial context, rubber flooring is tough and practical.

VINYL

In the early 1950s, vinyl was the new wonder flooring material; now it is as mainstream as suburbia. With the market dominated by designs that simulate other more expensive types of flooring, such as wood, tile and marble, the suburban associations can be hard to shake off. Away from the mainstream, however, there are plain solid colours as well as fresher, more contemporary designs that would suit a modern interior. Many of these are similar to industrial or contract vinyls, which incorporate chips, granules or flakes of filler to increase slip-resistance. Others are metallic, speckled or flecked with quartz that sparkles in the light.

Vinyl is wholly synthetic and contains a varying percentage of PVC, a thermoplastic, which gives the material flexibility. Designed to be practical, easy care and easy to fit in sheet or tile form, it is also relatively cheap. Even cheaper, and arguably more cheerful, are brightly coloured PVC runners and mats – ideal coverings for utility areas such as laundry rooms.

The basic finish is matt and grainy, but this can be waxed, and then buffed up to a glossy sheen.

Lino sheet is heavy and unwieldy and should be laid professionally. Cut designs are also a job for the expert. Tiles can be laid by an amateur, stuck with proprietary glue over a level base.

RUBBER

Studded rubber flooring made its first appearance in the home with the arrival of high-tech and, like the style itself, its period of popularity was somewhat brief. Now it is back again and seems set to gain a wider following, thanks to a much increased range of colours. Industrial

Below **Linoleum is once again a chic and respectable flooring material. A creative choice for kitchen floors especially, where its anti-bacterial properties are the most beneficial, it looks equally good cut into designs or simply laid as plain colour.**

Right **Although carpet comes far down the contemporary decorator's list of chosen floor coverings, it can look surprisingly modern, provided it has a subtly textured design and is used judiciously. Its warmth and softness are undeniable.**

Above **A thick pile, dewberry-coloured carpet, fitted the length of this large, open space, is as much a part of the colour scheme as the toning lilac and blue walls and ceiling. Its soft texture is matched by the fur on the Marcel Breuer chair.**

CARPET

The softest form of flooring is carpet. Warm and comfortable, it invites floor-level living: it is kind to bare feet and crawling babies; it is quiet, cushioned and easy to look after. Yet, while in many ways an ideal choice for a modern lifestyle, carpeting has lost ground to rather more inhospitable hard surfaces and, within the context of soft flooring, to more environmentally worthy natural floor coverings such as sisal and coir. This is in part due to carpet's reputation as a refuge for allergy-causing dust mites, in part due to the back-to-basics approach which favours ripping up carpet to reveal the bare boards underneath, but largely to do with the fact that carpet, once luxurious, is now safe and expected. Safest of all are those highly discreet, neutral colours and textures that were so favoured by modern architects and designers, such as charcoal grey industrial cord and flecked natural berbers.

Carpet, however, does not need to be boring. You can accentuate the sensuous element by choosing thick velvety cut pile in sumptuous ivory white or rich chocolate to create a mood of intimacy and enclosure, while outside the well-mannered neutral range, there are plenty of intense colours that would give any room a jolt of electricity. Shag pile is seriously fashionable again, while fake fur patterning shares a similar tongue-in-cheek aesthetic.

Faced with increasing competition from sisal, coir and jute, there are also 'natural' undyed wool carpets in the type of nubbly weaves reminiscent of the coarser plant fibre floor coverings, as well as self-coloured damask-like textures that combine tightly woven backgrounds with cut-and-loop relief designs. Like the blends of sisal and wood, these work well in bedrooms or areas of light traffic. The best carpets contain a high percentage of wool; synthetic fibres, such as acrylic, added to provide extra strength, bring down the price.

NATURAL FIBRE COVERINGS

Until relatively recently, most people's experience of floor coverings made of plant fibres was restricted to the bristly coir doormat or the ubiquitous bull's-eye rush matting, a favoured cheap flooring for studio apartments. All this has changed dramatically with the introduction of latex-backed wall-to-wall coverings which have made natural fibres such as sisal, coir, jute and seagrass as versatile as carpet.

Natural fibre coverings make classic neutral floors, understated enough to work well with strong contemporary furnishings, but with a forthright texture that offers more depth and character than carpet. Basic colours range from warm, golden honey tones to pale biscuit and off-white; there are also more strongly coloured, striped and patterned versions, particularly in

sisal, which is easiest to dye. Near-black or deep indigo sisal makes a graphic modern floor and a dramatic foil for rugs.

Overall, this family of materials has a fresh, simple, authentic look, which is good for creating a mood of informality. Some varieties are more overtly countrified, but most are sufficiently accommodating to make easy-going backdrops for contemporary interiors. Generally, however, natural fibres are not as comfortable underfoot as carpet and, without proper care or laid in the wrong situation, they may stain and wear unacceptably quickly.

Seagrass is smooth, tough and resists stains. Its very stain-resistance means it cannot be dyed, but some designs are available with coloured weft strings. Coir is rough and prickly; the basic weave is fairly rustic, but there are more sophisticated patterns featuring stripes or chevrons. Plaited rush matting has country-house overtones, but also works well in a more modern setting. None of these fibres is particularly suitable for stairs.

Sisal is the most versatile of all the natural fibres and the one with most decorative potential. Available in a range of colours and patterns, and blended with wool, it can be used throughout the home, except in kitchens, bathrooms and areas likely to become wet.

Jute coverings are the most modern in appearance, as well as the softest and least durable. Jute makes a refined, subtle floor for pared-down bedrooms and comes in a variety of weaves and colours, although the pale natural tones are most popular.

Below **Dust-free, neutral in colour and in keeping with a simple ethos, undyed sisal lends itself well to modern homes as a compromise between conventional carpet and bare floorboards. It is also the perfect background for brightly coloured rugs.**

RUGS

Rugs are perfect for injecting dramatic colour and pattern into sleek, modern interiors: they anchor furniture arrangement within fluid, open-plan spaces and deliver comfort where it is needed, without compromising the integrity of existing floor finishes.

In the contemporary interior, rugs have all the status of floor-level art, and there are many exciting and talented modern designers working in this field. Bold abstract patterns; calligraphic strokes of colour; naive, primitive designs – the diversity is as stimulating and provocative as anything you are likely to see hanging in an art gallery. Rugs by classic modern designers, such as Eileen Gray, are also still in production. Handmade or specially designed unique rugs from contemporary design showrooms tend to be extremely expensive, but there are many modern retail outlets with their own more modestly priced range of rugs.

Much less expensive, but often equally effective in a contemporary setting, are simple flatweave rugs from India and the Near East. Dhurries and kelims may be traditional hand-crafted products of these regions, but their fresh geometric designs are perfectly in tune with modern taste. Dhurries are usually made of cotton, while kelims are generally woollen. Western retailers working in conjunction with local weavers have introduced contemporary colourways to broaden their appeal.

For a more understated look, natural fibre coverings can be bound at the edges and laid loose as area rugs.

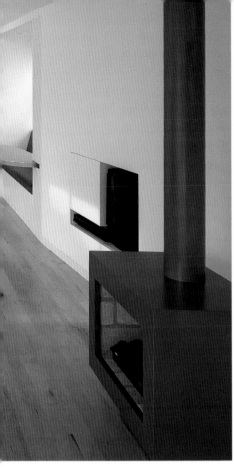

Left Rugs come into their own in large spaces. Here, a graphic union of orange and ochre makes heated reference to a wood-burning stove and introduces more colour.

Below Coir mats are effective at warming up rooms with exposed boards in winter. Bound at the edges, they introduce colour as well as textural interest at floor level.

Left Woven modernist rugs act in the same way as dramatic, abstract paintings, bringing colour and decoration to understated spaces. In this living area, the bold, geometric rug softens the sleek gloss of the wall-to-wall marble flooring.

Painted floorboards

Old, rustic floorboards can be given a contemporary facelift by sanding and filling them to a completely smooth surface. Painted a glossy pale grey, they will create a streamlined and sophisticated look in any room.

When preparing old floorboards for sanding or painting, scrub them first with a heavy brush and sugar soap (de-greaser). This will loosen any dirt and caked-on paint, stain or varnish, and help speed up the sanding process. If the floor has been waxed, the wax must be removed

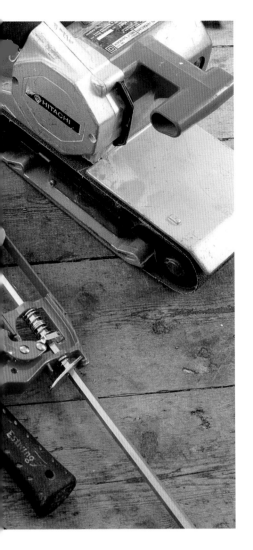

MATERIALS AND TOOLS

• Hammer • Nail punch • Belt sander • Edging sander • Resin filler and trigger-operated gun • Filling knife • Gloss paint and satin varnish, or matt paint and matt varnish

METHOD

1 Bang down any protruding nail heads with the hammer and nail punch until they are driven about 3mm (⅛in) below the level of the floor. If left proud of the surface, they will tear the sanding belt in the sander.

2 Initially, move the belt sander diagonally in both directions to smooth down any uneven or badly cupped floorboards. Then work along the length of the boards, following the grain of the wood, to avoid making scratches. Work from the outside of the room inwards, taking care that the sander does not touch the skirting boards (baseboards). Continue until the floorboards have an even finish and all traces of paint, varnish and stain have been removed. Then use the edging sander along the skirting boards. Vacuum the floor to gather up any dust.

3 Once the floor is smooth and clean, fill any gaps, holes or dents with resin filler. Apply with the gun and smooth over with a filling knife. Leave to dry.

Apply either the matt paint followed by a couple of layers of matt varnish, or the gloss paint followed by satin varnish. Allow each coat to dry before applying the next. The varnish will help to form a protective seal.

completely. Use wire wool soaked in white spirit and finish with a clean rag.

As sanders are expensive to buy, you may want to rent one. They are usually available by the day or weekend. Although sanding is time-consuming, the results are well worth the effort.

Although floor sanders have dust-extraction bags, they still produce a great deal of dust, so always wear a mask and old clothes. (Wear ear protectors, too.) Open any windows in the room and seal any doors with masking tape.

Hardboard tiling

This has to be one of the most economical ways of laying a smart new floor. While you could floor a whole room in this way, it is probably more suited to a smallish area – a workroom, for instance, or a narrow hallway. If your floorboards have seen better days and are uneven, tack down a sheet of standard hardboard over them before laying the hardboard tiles. The tiles are best pre-cut at a timber yard (lumberyard), usually from 2.5 x 1.2m (8 x 4ft) sheets. Ask for 28 x 28cm (11 x 11in) squares to allow for saw cuts and reduce wastage. The hardboard we used had been commercially treated with oil to provide a hardwearing surface.

MATERIALS AND TOOLS

• String • Sheets of oiled hardboard, 3mm (⅛in) thick, pre-cut into 28cm (11in) squares • Stanley knife or secateurs (clippers) • Hammer • Galvanized nails, 12mm (½in) long • Panel pins (brads) • Newspaper • Pencil • Steel rule • Sandpaper

METHOD

1 To find the centre of the floor area that you wish to cover (this will be where you position the centre of the first tile), run a piece of string from the centre point of one wall to the centre of the opposite wall. Do the same for the other two walls. Where the two pieces of strings cross is the centre. Mark it with a knot, drawing pin or tack. The piece of string running parallel to the longest wall is the line along which the first row of tiles should be laid in a diamond pattern. Lay the centre of the first tile under the knot.

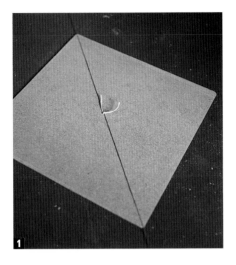

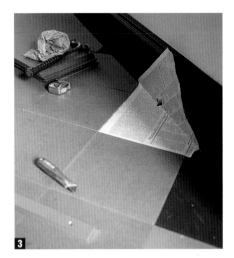

2 Nick off all four corners of each hardboard tile using a Stanley knife or secateurs (clippers). The nicks should be small enough for the head of the galvanized nail to rest on top of the tiny diamond shape you create when you place four tiles together. This prevents the tiles from being pushed apart when you bang in the nails and allows you to anchor four tiles with one nail. Radiate the tiles out from the central line, securing them as you go with galvanized nails. You can tack in some panel pins (brads) first to make sure the tiles stay in position.

3 The edging tiles will have to be cut to fit. Fold a page of newspaper to fit the remaining untiled area to make a template.

4 Lay the template on a tile and mark the shape of an edging tile with the pencil. With the steel rule and Stanley knife score a line on each side of the tile and snap off the excess. If the edge is not perfectly smooth, rub it with sandpaper. Follow the same procedure for all the edging tiles, securing them with galvanized nails.

Birch plywood flooring

This chic, contemporary floor has been created by slotting together wide boards of tongued-and-grooved birch plywood which are then coated with matt varnish. Measure your floor and decide how many standard lengths of board you need (plywood usually comes in 60 x 120cm/2 x 4ft boards). Your timber yard (lumberyard) should supply your exact requirements.

MATERIALS AND TOOLS

• String • Nail punch • Boards of tongued-and-grooved birch plywood • Matt varnish • Paint kettle • Hammer • Nails • Sandpaper • 10cm (4in) paintbrush

METHOD

After emptying the room of its contents, prepare the floor by knocking in any protruding nails with the punch and making sure the surface is smooth, dry and free of dust. (The advantage of laying a completely new floor over existing floorboards is that you do not have to worry too much about the condition of what you are covering up.) Then, find the centre of the floor by marking the middle point of the facing walls and stretching a piece of string between each of the two points. Where the two pieces of string cross is the centre of the floor. This is where the centre of the first board should be laid.

1 Lay down the first board in the centre of the room with its longest side parallel to the longest wall. Hammer in nails through the tongued side of the board at a 45-degree angle at 30cm (12in) intervals. In this way the nails will not get in the way of the adjacent boards and prevent them from butting up. The nails should be banged in so far that they are not visible and the board is securely held down. Once the first board is secure, continue laying down boards along the centre line, hammering in nails as you go. As it is very unlikely that the boards will be exactly the right size for your room, you will need to measure the shortfall between the walls and the last complete boards laid, and then cut boards to fit accordingly.

Once you have laid the centre line of boards, lay the rest of the boards in a 'brick' pattern either side of the centre line, offering up the grooved sides of the boards so that they slide into the tongued sides. You will probably need to hammer the boards into place but do so gently. Cut the edging boards to fit.

2 Apply several coats of matt varnish to protect the floor from dirt and scuff marks. Allow each coat to dry before applying the next.

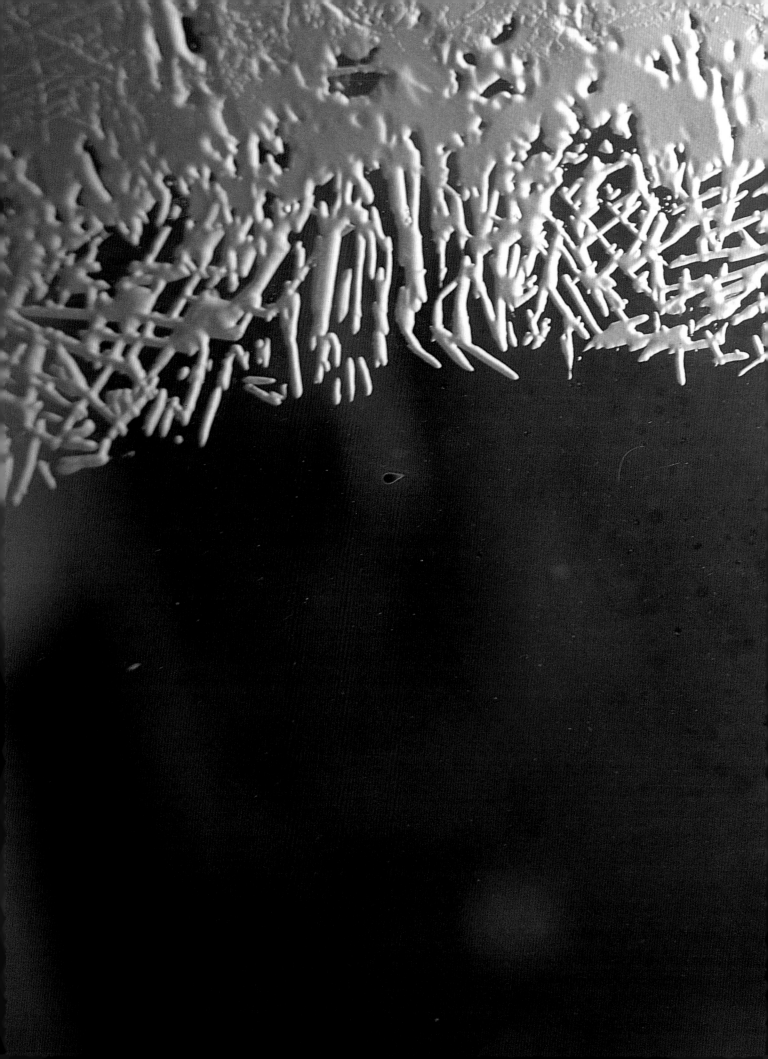

WINDOWS & DOORS

WINDOWS & DOORS

WINDOWS

Windows both preserve and broaden our space. They frame a view to the outside world, while providing a barrier between our public and private selves. Whatever the size of a room, its windows are a natural focal point, attracting the eye from within and without.

In the contemporary home, windows are often oversized and underdressed to maximize the natural light and so create an increased sense of space. One way of achieving this is to replace half-height windows with French windows; in addition to allowing more light into the room, French windows will also create an additional door to the outside. A more straight-forward and cheaper solution is to leave the window undressed except for a piece of fabric draped simply above the window, or to add just a pelmet, to give definition.

Windows that lead to balconies, patios, courtyards or directly onto grass or upwards, via a skylight, can be accentuated with fabric and colour so they both modulate the light and allow two different spaces – inside and outside – to merge into one another, creating an impression of generous proportions.

The entire mood of a room may be strongly influenced by the style of its windows, so it is important that their shape and material are sympathetic to the style and age of the building: windows with PVC frames may be practical but in a period home they will look totally out of place.

As new, large windows are likely to upset the natural symmetry of a building if its other windows are of a different style, mullions aping

the style of existing windows in the same room can be added. These will break up the big expanse of glass, thereby softening its impact.

Huge areas of glass can waste energy if they are not carefully fitted, allowing heat to be lost instead of harnessed. To help overcome this problem, many contemporary architects are experimenting with natural solar power and using it as a principal energy source in the home.

DOORS

In the contemporary home, doors have a versatile role. As well as forming the link between two separate room spaces, they also act as temporary dividers, rather like screens (see also Walls, page 35). The common practice of

Above Neat and unobtrusive sliding doors provide easy access from a bedroom to an adjoining bathroom. When closed, the simple beech frames and frosted panels create an opaque division between the two rooms.

Left The recessed windows in this tranquil bathroom are so tall and narrow that neither curtains nor blinds are needed to ensure complete privacy. Uninterrupted light also flows in through the skylight.

Above **The distinction between window and door is blurred in a space divided by integral glass bricks and a single sliding plywood panel. The dining area can be opened out onto the rest of the room, enabling light to stream in from the external window.**

'knocking through' a room to enlarge a living space is the simplest way of increasing the amount of light and air in a home. The division can be marked with glazed doors, or concertina-style plywood doors that are either left undecorated or inlaid with corrugated plastic, Formica strips or steel mesh.

A sliding door will both divide and open up a room, allowing more living space while still retaining the feeling of two separate areas, and 'fluid' doors, such as bead curtains or fabric drapes, will demarcate spaces or rooms without making a firm division of function. And there is always the ribbon door curtain which no self-respecting 1960s kitchen was without. Practical for discouraging insects and filtering sunlight while allowing cool breezes, children and pets to come and go, ribbon doors add colour, light and air to doorways and other openings, bringing with them a touch of the kasbah.

In modern decorating, doors often merge seamlessly into walls in a uniformity of colour and texture. Plywood-panelled walls, for example, can appear as an unbroken run when doors are made of plywood, too, and the door furniture is understated. Similarly, glass doors that open out onto a walled courtyard will allow interior and exterior spaces to merge into one.

However, in the airy contemporary home, where rooms are larger and walls and doors fewer, doors can become dramatic features in their own right. But their proportions should not disturb those of windows and features elsewhere in the room. Doors that make their own statement, acting as focal points, or creating

Left Instant light effects are created with a bead curtain screening a metallic-finished glass door. Set against a fur rug, the overall effect is shiny, smart and stylish.

Below The pure harmony of white on white is difficult to beat, especially when doors and openings are seamlessly integrated into walls. A tiny kitchenette has been cleverly recessed into this curved landing wall.

strong demarcation or punctuation in a room, can be fashioned from a range of materials. Natural doors of tightly packed bamboo canes or salvaged wood such as floorboards make striking room dividers and bring an element of surprise into a space. A setting that embraces industrial chic will be enhanced with zinc-clad swing doors or MDF (particleboard) doors that have a tight steel mesh cut into them.

Movable doors made of frosted glass panels on slim metal castors cast a glorious warm glow back and forth between the divided spaces when they are closed at night. Alternative panels can be created from sheets of calico stretched over a wooden framework; zinc or aluminium sheeting for a warehouse aesthetic; or tiny mosaic squares applied to a wooden base for a touch of colour. A number of pivoting floor-to-ceiling screens with curved

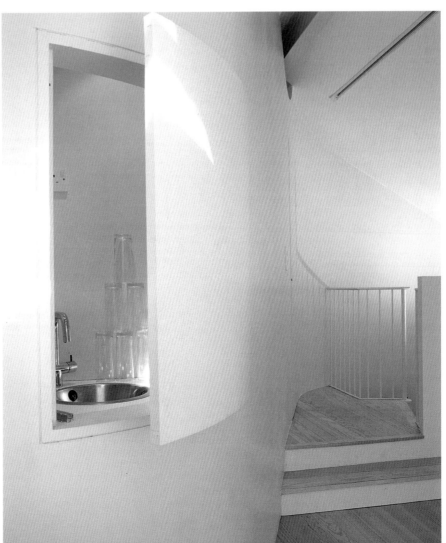

plywood facings make dramatic doors which, when closed, form a movable 'wall' of wood. Sliding door panels can be fitted with oversized chrome handles or small steel knobs according to the emphasis you want to place on them.

The traditional door, fashioned from hardwood, panelled and finished with brass knobs can be entirely reinterpreted for the contemporary interior. To reinforce the ethos of clean lines and rich texture, use simple plywood panels punctuated around the outer edges with clout nails (tacks); their shiny surfaces can be echoed with a streamlined chrome dormitory handle. Specially created doors, shaped from MDF (particleboard) or plywood, are versatile additions to a room, extending the decorative theme or making a dramatic statement between spaces. The pliability of these materials means they can be easily shaped with a jigsaw to produce, for example, a porthole. A variation on the saloon door can be made by cutting wavy shapes at the top and bottom of a door, or by piercing a full-length door with squares, circles or crosses for a geometric look.

Aluminium sheeting laid in panels on a plywood base and lightly burnished creates an air of industrial chic. Reinforced safety glass or a frosted panel are more elegant alternatives. For the ultimate in smart room transitions, a strong glass door on double-jointed hinges and embellished with steel handles in organic shapes is both light-giving and a bold, clean statement. But such a choice should be very carefully considered if there are small children in the home.

Corrugated polyethylene is a light, versatile and cheap material to experiment with. Reinforced with a mesh system, it can be used to make a complete door. Alternatively, use classic Formica laid over plywood.

Plain doors in beech, cherrywood, bleached ash or simple ply or MDF (particleboard) can look extremely chic, especially if the door furniture is apposite, understated or contrasting.

To play with scale, place oversized handles at a slightly lower height for dramatic impact, or attach tiny steel handles discreetly at the vertical edge of the door. Use solid wood wedges or curved handles, chrome door pulls or coloured glass knobs for a touch of contrast; try small chrome knobs. You can even take a length of thick chandler's rope and knot it through a circle that has been sawn in the door.

Left **Square glass bricks and round holes punctuate walls and doors in an airy kitchen. The doors are painted the same colour as the kitchen units to enhance the sense of space, while the glass bricks are both light providers and room divider.**

Above **Gently curving, Japanese-style sliding doors with beech frames screen a bathroom space. The floor tiles and square-shaped cupboard beneath the marble sink echo the proportions of the screen for a considered effect.**

Above **Rectangles of coloured sugar paper fixed to panes of glass, chequerboard-style, interrupt the view but create luminous patterns of deep pink and turquoise blue light on the walls and window ledge.**

qualities do away with the need for further window treatments, and it can be applied equally well to windows and doors, filtering the light in a particularly pleasing manner.

Opaque glass, introduced in the form of frosted panes, is elegant and provides privacy without a reduction in light. Although fairly costly, these panes can be used sparingly. Fitted in the bottom half of a street-facing window, for instance, they will block the view of inquisitive passers-by, but not the daylight. Glass etched with spots, stripes, lettering or abstract designs will break up the surface and provide

GLAZING

Standard glazing for windows and doors can be replaced with or tempered by a wide range of materials to vary the amount of light let into a room. At the cheap and simple end of the chain is heavyweight artists' tracing paper. Fixed to window frames over the existing glazing with galvanized clout nails or gold or chrome-coloured metal drawing pins (tacks), it brings instant opacity for a tiny outlay. Another economical variation of *faux* glazing is self-adhesive coloured vinyl sheeting. Available in a vast range of colours, it allows you flexibility with your decorative scheme. Its opaque and light-reflecting

interesting plays of light for front doors and bathroom windows. Unfortunately, etched designs are rather expensive and should probably be reserved for small areas.

Old coloured and textured glass is often to be found at salvage yards or specialist glass suppliers. Traditionally used in stained-glass panels for doors and transoms or as small corner details in windows, coloured glass has also been reinterpreted for the modern idiom. Sunlight dancing through a pane of coloured glass creates marvellous kaleidoscopic tones in a contemporary room.

Glass bricks (see Walls, pages 36–7) and corrugated polyethylene (see page 77) can also be used for glazing. For some internal doors that do not have a soundproofing role, glazing may be deemed unnecessary. A porthole shape, for example, can be left unglazed; alternatively, it can be covered with steel mesh to create an industrial feel. Chicken wire or stretched canvas are other options.

On a practical note, toughened, shatter-proof glass is an absolute must for French windows, large patio doors and internal doors that children use regularly.

Above **Half-height panes of glass fixed in front of the windows for extra security have been spray-frosted for privacy. A decorative porthole has been left in the middle, the frosting scratched off randomly around the circumference to create a snowflake effect.**

Left **All-white walls highlighted with cobalt blue accessories give this period bedroom a cool and contemporary look. The etched human figures on the stained glass door panels provide a softening effect.**

WINDOW TREATMENTS

Today's homes demand as much light as possible. Contemporary window dressing is the art of understatement. Crisp, clean and utterly economical, modern window treatments often combine a number of approaches, mixing Venetian blinds with sheer curtains or roller blinds with ultra simple headings for crisp but effective solutions.

While there is a case for leaving windows untreated in a contemporary scheme, the need for privacy and warmth can override a strictly minimal approach unless you happen to live in a warm climate, where you are not overlooked or the views from within are exceptional and calming. Fabulous countryside and soothing seascapes demand to be seen, day and night.

To some extent, the shape of a window dictates the way in which you should screen your view. Porthole windows are striking left bare, and you can always steal a glimpse through them. Deep arched windows are also best left alone, or else covered completely at night with floor-to-ceiling drapes. Simple sheets of sheer fabric suit large picture windows because they have a softening effect on a big expanse of glass, while more traditional sashes and casements will benefit from roller or Roman blinds, fitting neatly into the frame and making pleasing graphic shapes.

The twentieth-century modernist guru Le Corbusier expressed a preference for stark white and Venetian blinds at the window. However, while still adhering to the minimalist maxim, today's designers of domestic interiors are less rigorous in their application of accepted modern design principles. Indeed, many contemporary decorators crave a less rigid devotion to seriously stark windows, particularly in rooms where the flooring is made of concrete or wood. Such rooms require a higher degree of acoustic cushioning than those that have carpets and natural floor coverings. This is easily and effectively provided by curtains and blinds, as well as soft furnishings.

Left Simple, understated roller blinds continue the clean lines of this rectilinear space. Pulled down to varying heights, they screen the view and filter the bright sunlight.

Far left A chrome pole makes an inconspicuous curtain rail for four banner curtains. Eyelets have been inserted across a simple heading so that the curtains can be threaded onto the pole, allowing them to be pulled into a variety of configurations.

Below Wooden Venetian blinds are an elegant choice for sash windows. Pulled up, they reveal the pleasing proportions of older-style window frames. Choose a wood or wood colour that is sympathetic to your furniture.

CURTAINS

Contemporary curtains are cool, colourful and breezy, breathing light and air into a room. They no longer hang heavily in huge swathes of inter-lined chintz topped with fiddly, fussy headings and draped with tassels and tie-backs. These days, windows are more likely to feature simple metal poles hung with several layers of muslin in shades such as fuchsia, indigo and saffron. Fabrics that communicate colour, cultural diversity and a sense of movement make bold, intriguing combinations against a scrupulously white window. Texture is often more important than pattern, especially if it complements smooth surfaces elsewhere in the room. Loud rose-covered bowers are supplanted by more subtle patterns and motifs such as geometrics, formal stripes and miniature florals.

HEADINGS, POLES AND PELMETS

There are many ways of avoiding the predictability of the wooden curtain pole finished at each end with a bulbous finial. Among the many options for contemporary poles there is a simple chrome rail hung with café clips or steel rings, a galvanized steel scaffolding tube, polyester rope over brass pulleys, ceiling-hung metal hooks, curtain wire, bamboo poles, wooden dowels and chrome or copper tubing.

Curtains have a tendency to hang boldly from slimline poles, or from nails, to resemble wall-hangings. Fabric stiffly attached to a runner with invisible hooks looks overdressed. Many curtains include integral headings and fixings, such as stiffened curtain fabric punched with nickel eyelets, or simple tied headings in the

Below left **Muslin hangs in loose gathers from a wrought-iron pole that has been fixed at either end of the bedroom wall. The muslin is clipped into thin rings which glide lightly along the pole.**

Below right **Colour and abundance in the form of an indigo and turquoise curtain trailing pleasingly on the floor is offset against plain painted walls and a slim chrome pole fitted into the window recess.**

same or contrasting fabric. Cased headings will thread straight on to a pole. Curtains can also be attached directly to a window frame with metal 'turn' buttons. Pull the curtain back during the day by hooking it over a steel hold-back or tucking it in a tie-back.

Despite being traditionally associated with overblown window treatments, pelmets can play a valid part in a contemporary decorating scheme. Plywood or MDF (particleboard) pelmets in a straightforward box shape, or perhaps sawn into wavy lines, or even with graphic notches, supply extra definition and interest for very simple window treatments. They will also become focal points in their own right. Modern materials, such as Perspex (Plexiglas), zinc or aluminium, are also exciting to experiment with above simply dressed windows.

Left **Simple in the extreme, this crumpled muslin curtain is suspended from café clips on heavy-duty cord, which is weighted at both ends with a piece of stone.**

Above **Floor-to-ceiling windows are complemented by discreet white roller blinds tucked neatly into the ceiling recess of this pure white and wood bedroom.**

BLINDS

Depending on the style of the other furnishings in a room, blinds can often replace curtains. They work extremely well combined with other blinds or lightweight drapes of muslin, calico or scrim. Economic versions include the simple bamboo or paper blind.

Roller blinds can be as straightforward as a piece of thick calico, hand-rolled onto a length of wooden dowelling and suspended with thick chandler's rope, or as sophisticated as strong canvas applied to steel and fixed with a smooth-flowing cord mechanism. Within limitations shop-bought blinds can be customized to fit your windows, but for more awkward spaces or more complicated systems, you will have to order tailor-made blinds.

For large windows, think about commissioning double blinds made from two different fabrics – sheer on top and opaque below – so that the light is not shut out but privacy is guaranteed. Alternatively, fit reverse roller blinds that pull up from the bottom of the window – neat and very effective (see pages 92–3). Blinds made of tough white cotton with squares and circles cut into them allow the light to permeate, while muslin, treated with fabric stiffener, can be used for lightweight roller blinds. Bound edges provide definition and textural variety, especially if contrasting colours are used.

Roman blinds are a softer alternative to the streamlined roller blind. Gathered in deep or narrow folds and made from cool calico, they bring Zen-like calm to an all-white scheme. By varying the fabric, using rich, deep colours

Left **Recessed windows are the ideal setting for Roman blinds, which lend some softness to the strictly regular lines in this living room.**

Below **In a converted warehouse, where the windows are large and non-standard shapes, custom-made Venetian blinds are a good idea. Being overlooked is never an issue with this form of window treatment.**

or dramatic geometric prints, Roman blinds can be made into much more of a feature. As the sole window covering they are at once simple and introduce warmth to a room, but they also make great backdrops for window drapes or conventional curtains.

The choice of true minimalists, Venetian blinds are the answer for all sizes of window. Steel, wood and plastic versions are available in a large variety of colours and slat sizes, either custom-made or in standard widths and lengths. Venetian blinds are functional, flexible and elegant, allowing several ways of screening and filtering light. They are especially useful in kitchens and bathrooms where light levels need to be varied throughout the day and, like other blinds, work well on their own or in conjunction with other window coverings.

Fabrics

Neutral or natural, stripes or bold geometrics, the fabrics and textures favoured by modern decorators are brave, new, and a world away from the stuffy chintz and brocades of the last century that have persisted in popularity. In contemporary decorating, fabrics are chosen for their integrity and impact rather than any visual reference to specific furnishing styles.

Texture was deemed to be paramount in textile design during the post-Bauhaus years. But the machine aesthetic meant that many of the fabrics produced on power looms lacked the open-weave, authentic texture offered by hand-woven examples. This dilemma resulted in many leading designers – Jack Lenor Larsen, Dorothy Liebes and the Knoll fabric division in the United States – experimenting with producing fabrics in wool, jute fibres and metallic Lurex that had a hand-loomed look.

Geometric designs are both classic and contemporary; they also age well and make a striking graphic addition to a modern room. Multi-coloured circles, squares and zigzags are currently enjoying a revival in the decorating world, thanks to a renewed interest in Swedish and English textiles of the 1950s. In contrast, understated sorbet-coloured ginghams and ultra-stylized floral prints, which conjure up distant childhood memories, introduce a soft note to a contemporary decorating scheme.

Stripes have also been rediscovered, replacing checks as the 'must-have' fabric for window treatments. They range from bold and daring blocks of shockingly bright colours to

Below **Semi-sheer banner curtains bearing an abstract design are reminiscent of Scandinavian fabrics of the 1950s. In a space that mixes modern materials in a forthright manner, the fabric captures and enhances the style of the architecture.**

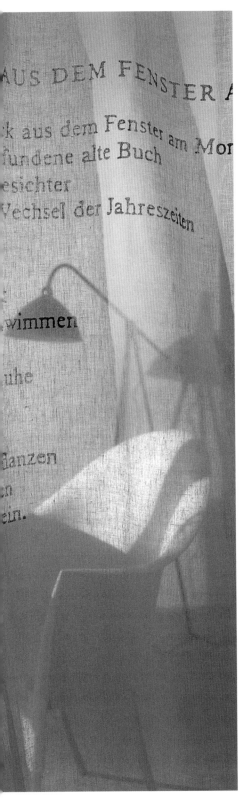

subtler Regency-style combinations of deep blues and reds. Natural cotton ticking in myriad colours is both natural and crisply contemporary, fulfilling the twin desires of an ecological as well as pared-down approach to decoration.

For the ever-popular, all-white look, nothing can beat sheer butter muslin or pre-shrunk calico. Calico is an excellent fabric for Roman blinds, roller blinds and 'instant' draped or pinned curtains, while silks and organzas in neutral tones provide a floaty, luxurious texture in an otherwise taut scheme.

In a generous space, such as a converted warehouse apartment, a dramatic approach works well. Large 'drops' of coloured vinyl, the sort most commonly used for shower curtains, are almost essential for huge warehouse

Above **Straw-coloured cotton is smartened with two rows of horizontal plum stripes, just below sill height. Stripes can also be added along vertical edges and at the top of curtains for graphic definition. Use them to echo colours elsewhere in a room.**

Left **Ethereal muslin sheers demarcate an area and make an esoteric statement, in the most literal sense of the word, with a poem by Bertolt Brecht: 'The First Look out of the Window in the Morning'.**

Above **Muslin and calico combine to provide neutral window treatments in a room flooded with natural light. Economic and elegant, these materials can be used at any window in any kind of scheme.**

windows. Vinyl comes in a huge range of bold colours or just plain opaque. Thicker versions can also be fashioned into practical roller blinds for kitchens and bathrooms.

Everyday materials should not be overlooked either. Simple wrappings such as brown paper, tracing paper and tea towels can all be transformed into inexpensive and effective window coverings or blinds. Treated with stiffener, they become stylish shoestring solutions for a contemporary decorator. Thick bubblewrap is another option.

An element of kitsch plays a part in some contemporary schemes. Over-grandiose curtain drapes in velvet, silk and organza combined with huge gilt mirrors, chandeliers and fake fur provide an interesting tension when used in conjunction with modern streamlined furniture.

New fabrics are being researched all the time; some of the most interesting are solar materials. Backed with aluminium powder, they reflect light and heat in summer but retain it in winter, combining energy conservation with clean good looks.

SHUTTERS

Shutters cut out light, draughts and noise. Comforting on cold winter evenings, they are also cool sun shades for the summer. Contemporary shutters make use of different materials to look new and exciting. Shaped plywood, Perspex (Plexiglas) panels and zinc-plated MDF (particleboard) are all possibilities, in addition to the classic louvred wood design. Try detachable versions that can be unhooked and propped decoratively in a room by day.

While metal shuttering is most often found in hot countries where the heat of the day needs to be kept at bay, it can work well in scrupulously styled rooms or spaces where the view is simply not worth having.

Above In an elegant room where the original wooden shutters, architraves and floorboards remain, the architectural detail has been left to speak for itself.

Left When is a shutter not a shutter? When it doubles as a Venetian blind and is a decorative element in its own right.

Frosted glazing

By rendering glazed windows and doors translucent rather than completely opaque, privacy can be maintained while only a minimum amount of natural light is blocked. Unfortunately, this usually involves a hefty investment in hand-etched or sandblasted glass. However, with a spray can of glass frosting, available from artists' suppliers, or a can of clear matt varnish, available from hardware stores, and the judicious placing of stationery labels and stickers, few people would be able to tell the difference between the art of a master craftsperson and a crafty contemporary decorator.

Random or regular patterns can be achieved with sticky labels in all manner of sizes and shapes, from ovals, oblongs and stars to mini-targets made from paper reinforcers. Strips of masking tape or double-sided tape can be stuck down in cross formations. Alternatively, you can make your own motifs from cardboard by drawing simple shapes with a pencil and marker pen, placing the card on a cutting mat, then cutting them out with a scalpel (craft knife). Stick the motifs on the glass with double-sided tape and be as imaginative as you please: create graphic coastal waves or a simple porthole shape on a bathroom door, or geometric shapes on a front door. You can even design a stylized landscape or add chunky lettering that looks hand-etched. If you have an unpleasant view out of a casement window, the frosting can be applied, unbroken, to the bottom few panes.

As it is quite difficult to remove marks from the frosting, try to spray on the side of the glass that is less likely to be touched.

MATERIALS AND TOOLS

- Masking tape • Stationery stickers or labels
- Can of spray frosting or clear matt varnish
- Scalpel (craft knife)

METHOD

1 Mask off all areas of the door surrounding the glass that is to be sprayed. We used specialist decorating masking tape, but ordinary masking tape and paper will work just as well. Lightly apply the stationery stickers to form a pattern. (It is a good idea to experiment beforehand on a separate piece of paper if you have a particular configuration in mind.)

2 Following the manufacturer's instructions, apply the frosting spray in even strokes over the area to be covered. Make sure the can is held at the same distance from the glass surface at all times, and always finish off a stroke on the masking paper and not on the glass to prevent blobs of frosting forming. When the frosting is dry, gently peel off the stickers with a scalpel.

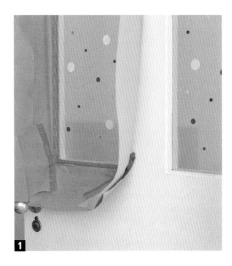

Pull-up roller blinds

This neat variation on the everyday roller blind replaces curtains in an airy, uncluttered living room. The advantage that these 'upside-down' blinds has over conventional roller blinds is that they act as screens, providing privacy, but at the same time they allow in as much natural light as possible at the top half of the window.

The blinds are made from lightweight but durable nylon kite fabric, which is subtly textured and easy to work with. (For a roller blind, it is essential to use a lightweight material, but for a simple drape or banner you could experiment with heavier fabrics.) The fabric is attached to a conventional roller blind kit, available from department stores. We have used white fabric for our blinds, but it does come in many colours. Once the blind is made, handle it carefully to stop it from being marked.

MATERIALS AND TOOLS

• Nylon kite fabric • Marker pen • Straightedge • Dressmaker's scissors • Thumbtacks • Staple gun and staples • One roller blind kit per window • Bradawl • Screwdriver • L-shaped screw hooks

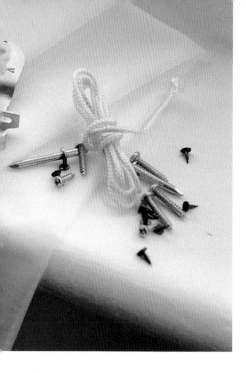

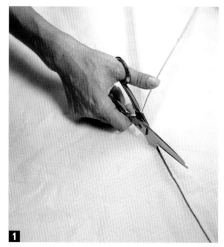

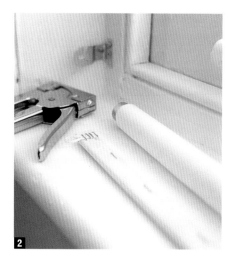

METHOD

Calculate the amount of fabric you need by measuring the window space you want to cover, then adding 8cm (3in) at both the top and bottom to allow for 'hems'. Make sure that the fabric you buy is wide enough for your windows; the kite fabric we used comes in 150cm (5ft) widths, which is plenty wide enough for generously proportioned casement windows such as these.

1 Lay the kite fabric on a large, flat surface such as a table or workbench. Mark the required length and width in straight lines on the fabric using a straightedge and marker pen. Be sure to use proper dressmaker's scissors to cut the fabric; although durable, it is rather thin and liable to stretch if cut carelessly and tugged about too much.

2 Once you have cut it to fit, turn the fabric under 12mm (½in) at one end and tack, glue or staple it onto the wooden dowel part of the roller blind kit. Wind the fabric around the dowel. When you reach the other end of the fabric, turn in the selvage and tuck it around the wooden

batten. Secure the fabric with staples at 5cm (2in) intervals. At either end of the batten form a cord loop (cord is supplied with the roller blind kit) and secure with staples. These will anchor the blind to the window frame.

Mark the positions of the blind fixings on the window frame with a marker pen and use a straightedge or spirit level to check that they are straight and line up with each other. Secure the fixings to the window frame with a bradawl and screwdriver.

3 Slip the dowel and blind mechanism into the slots, making sure that the blind rolls outwards towards you – this looks much neater.

4 Pull up the blind and mark the position of the L-shaped screw hooks with a marker pen that has been slipped through the loops at each end of the blind. Make a pilot hole with a bradawl, then screw the hooks into the window frame. Hang the blind on the hooks with the cord loops.

Folding window shutters

Shutters are a stylish alternative to curtains in a contemporary room. Elegant and practical, these plain-panelled, folding shutters made from Perspex (Plexiglas) are clean-lined as well as simple to make, maintain and use. Although a rather unconventional material to have at the window, Perspex is very versatile, allowing light into the room yet providing privacy.

Pre-cut Perspex is available from sign-makers and specialist hardware stores. Unlike some contemporary materials, it is not cheap. However, it would cost no more to make these shutters than it would to make and fit a Roman blind or buy a ready-made Venetian blind.

If you want bright colours at the window and are prepared to pay a lot more money, you could try fluorescent Perspex, which concentrates most of the light at the edge of the sheet to create a warm glow around the window. Complete opacity can be achieved with plywood, MDF (particleboard) or hardwood.

MATERIALS AND TOOLS

To make two shutters, each of two panels:
• Metal tape measure • Four sheets of 6mm (¼in) thick Perspex (Plexiglas), cut to fit • Straightedge • Marker pen • Hand drill • 16 face-fixing (butterfly) hinges, 2.5cm (1in) long • 48 nuts, bolts and washers • 16 wood screws • Pliers • Screwdriver

METHOD

Measure the length and width of your window. To calculate the width of each panel, divide the width of the window by four and subtract 3cm

(1¼in) – this allows a gap of 6mm (¼in) between each panel for the hinges, and a gap of the same size between the two shutters when they are closed. Both shutters should fit within the window area without any light filtering through at the top or bottom. Ask your supplier to cut the Perspex to the right size.

1 Lay two panels of Perspex on a hard, flat surface, such as a large piece of scrap wood, or clamp them onto a workbench. Align the top and bottom of both panels along a straightedge. Move the panels 6mm (¼in) apart to accommodate the hinges, and mark the position of each hinge and bolt hole with the marker pen. The top and bottom hinges should be no less than 15cm (6in) away from the top and bottom edges of the panels, and the middle two hinges should be positioned at an equal distance between them.

With the hand drill make bolt holes for the top hinges of both panels. Remove the backing from the Perspex. Attach the top hinges with nuts, bolts and washers before securing the bottom hinges. (Use pliers to steady the nuts and washers while screwing in the bolts.) Bolt in the middle hinges and those that will fix onto the window frame. For the latter, the distance from the centre pin of the hinge to the edge of the Perspex should be 6mm (¼in).

Attach the hinges to the other two panels in the same way.

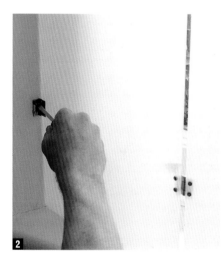

2 Once all the hinges are attached, stand two joined panels in the window space, with the hinges facing outwards, to establish the correct position of the hinges on the window frame. Use the straightedge to ensure the screw holes for the hinges on the frame line up with those on the shutter, and mark their position with the marker pen. Remove the Perspex while drilling a pilot hole in the frame. Reposition the panel and screw the hinges onto the frame. Repeat for the other half of the shutter.

FURNITURE & FURNISHINGS

FURNITURE & FURNISHINGS

Furniture, along with fixtures and fittings, brings the contemporary look into focus. Concentrating on the products of modern design to equip and furnish your home may at first seem like a narrowing of options. But what was once a limited field, and in some respects an expensive one, offers great scope today in terms not only of appearance and function, but also of affordability. As well as the high-profile classics by famous designers, there is a huge range of good-looking contemporary furnishings available from mass-market outlets that falls well within the budget of the average household. Recycled pieces of utility furniture from other contexts, such as shops, schools and factories, increase the choice still further.

Modern furniture conjures up images of those severe pieces in black leather and chrome that dominated the 'international style' phase of modernism in the immediate postwar years: a look more reminiscent, perhaps, of the corporate lobby than the living room. But a glance at any contemporary collection, in a design showroom or even design museum, tells a very different story. Organic shapes, brilliant colour, the sympathetic and innovative use of materials are equally definitive, from the sublime curves of Jacobsen's Egg chair to Zanotta's inflatable see-through armchair.

And if modern furniture can be fun, it can also be comfortable. Simplicity and functionalism need not rule out the human element; in fact, furniture that does not accommodate the body is not functioning well. Some design icons of the twentieth century do have a reputation

for being far from comfortable, but many more are the product of sophisticated and sensitive research into the posture of the human form and how best to support it.

A key element of contemporary furnishing is flexibility. Chairs that fold or stack, stools that serve as seats or tables, low units on wheels for mobile storage bring the potential for multi-functioning to multi-purpose spaces.

Left **Seamless glass shelves ranged across a stainless steel splashback and resting on chrome supports create an easy-access store cupboard for kitchen essentials.**

Below **Funky, space-age, purple chairs are both organic and inviting. An accompanying floor lamp is equally appealing, casting a tower of light up and against yellow walls.**

Above **An inspired mix of old, new and neutral looks crisp and contemporary. Bentwood café chairs sit alongside pared-down metal tables, while the floorboards are covered with sheets of thick plywood for an air of casual chic.**

TYPES OF FURNITURE

The contemporary furniture market ranges from classic modern pieces by famous designers such as Alvar Aalto, Corbusier, Charles Eames, Arne Jacobsen and Marcel Breuer to the simple anonymous products of chain-store retailers, taking in along the way survivors from previous incarnations of modernism – such as 1950s flying saucer chairs – which turn up second-hand at junk shops and markets. And, over the past decade, the range has been broadened still further by the work of contemporary designers, from star names such as Philippe Starck to lesser-known but often equally exciting young graduates producing the classics of the future.

Anyone who has ever been inspired by the spirit of modernism has probably experienced a desire to own one or more of the famous twentieth-century landmarks of design. For a long while, pieces such as Le Corbusier's chaise longue (now known to have been designed by his associate Charlotte Perriand), his Grand Confort armchair, Mies van der Rohe's Barcelona chair, the Eames chair and the like have had an elite following that has kept them in small-scale but more or less continuous production. Many such designs were intended originally to be mass-produced like Thonet's bentwood café chairs, at one time so ubiquitous as to be almost generic. But because modernism remained a minority enthusiasm for much of this century, designs such as the Corbusier armchair have become highly visible status symbols. Originals command high prices at auction; even new versions, produced under licence, are expensive.

Other classic modern designs that have recently enjoyed a new lease of life include furniture by the great Scandinavian designers Arne Jacobsen and Alvar Aalto. Jacobsen's

curving, colourful chairs such as the Egg and the Swan are beautiful expressions of organic modernity, while the moulded Butterfly chair, in brilliant rainbow shades, has almost become a contemporary cliché. Not as high profile, but nonetheless incredibly versatile, is the classic Aalto stacking stool – either a seat or a table for bedside or chairside.

At the opposite end of the spectrum, both in terms of price and celebrity, are the contemporary ranges available from modern retailers. It has never been so easy or so economical to buy modern. Long, low and laidback sofas, stacking and folding chairs in aluminium or

slatted wood, metal café tables, plywood easy chairs with webbed seats, glass dining tables on metal frameworks, tubular steel bedsteads – the list of options is ever-increasing. With a clarity of form and line that is mixed with a Scandinavian-style sympathy for material, such designs bring a refreshing sense of understatement to the home.

At the cutting edge, the work of new modern designers is gaining increased prominence. Furniture fairs are good places to spot up-and-coming talent. Witty and innovative designs in brave new materials such as polypropylene, recycled plastic, compressed paper and neoprene challenge traditional ideas of form and function. 'Transformative' furniture – such as chairs that turn into cupboards or pack away as bags – dissolve the conventional boundaries of furniture types and uses.

While high-tech may be dead, the recycling spirit lives on. Secondhand shops, markets and salvage companies are good sources of utility furniture and fittings that might once have equipped schools, hospitals, shops, offices or factories. Tubular steel and canvas stacking chairs from church halls, metal dentist's cabinets, medical trolleys, filing cabinets and lockers, glazed display cabinets from outfitters all make handsome additions to the contemporary look. Any piece that displays simple lines can be revamped with paint for a fresh, modern look. Applying sheets of other materials – such as Perspex (Plexiglas) or zinc to a tabletop (see also pages 116–17) – can accentuate the contemporary dimension.

Above Versatile and simple, this long, low sofa is sufficiently large to double as a bed. Huge cushions and a thin but firm mattress lend warmth and softness, the wooden frame is reassuring and the whole piece blends effortlessly with the stripped floor and neutral walls.

BACK TO BASICS

It is not necessary to be a fully paid-up minimalist to appreciate the benefits of spaciousness. In a crowded world, space – empty space – is the ultimate soother. At home, putting things back into perspective means avoiding tiresome clutter and redundant detail, and concentrating on what is essential. Essential furnishings are not merely functional in the strict practical sense: rather, they are furnishings that contribute positively to the ease and enjoyment of life.

Contemporary furnishing is not about updating traditional pieces of furniture with modern equivalents: it means taking a look at the functions a space must fulfil and providing the means for these to be achieved. In the private domains of the home, such as the bedrooms, the strategy of simplicity can pay striking dividends. A great bed, a clear floor and soft light make a refuge from stresses and strains. In living areas, the same applies. Comfortable seating, good lighting, a table for eating or working provide the starting point. This fundamental attitude not only encourages a paring down of possessions and furnishings but provides a basic coherence throughout all areas of the home.

MIXING AND MATCHING

The contemporary interior is spare rather than cluttered, with space defined by loose groupings and arrangements of furniture to serve different functions. But where less is more, each

Below **Only essential pieces of furniture are in place in this well-structured living area, which exudes light and comfort. Decoration is correspondingly minimal.**

piece must work twice as hard and the ensemble has to be harmonious and effortless. 'Big name' pieces scattered thinly on the ground will look more like a design museum than a home; on the other hand, a minimal and discreet collection of furnishings can run the risk of being a little dull and uninspired. The answer is to mix one-offs with collections, and play with scale, proportion and shape to create a dynamic mix.

Recognizably famous designs can be attention-seeking. A room full of such pieces can be a clamorous place, where the eye cannot choose between one statement and the next. It is often more effective to set off a single signature design with anonymous, clean-lined furniture as a working backdrop.

Simple furniture that comes in a series can be very useful for creating a sense of continuity. Aalto stools – or their lookalikes – provide versatile surfaces around the home. Plain functional chairs, such as director's chairs, Hans Coray's aluminium chairs, folding or slatted café chairs, make unobtrusive partners for a dining table or as additional, mobile seating in a living area.

Scale is also important. In the average home, one of the largest pieces of furniture is likely to be the sofa. A big sofa is a comfort zone of the first order, but its size and bulk can also be a useful way of anchoring furniture arrangement in an airy open space. Squashy, padded shapes have given way to cleaner lines, unfussy covering and exposed legs. In a restrained, rectilinear setting, the sweeping asymmetric curve of a sofa back introduces movement, while vibrant upholstery provides a colourful accent.

Juxtaposing materials gives a depth of character to contemporary furnishing. In living spaces, you could blend upholstered seating with metal occasional tables; in dining areas, try out combinations such as a wooden table with metal dining chairs or a glass table with wooden chairs – simplicity of form gains vitality from a mix of materials.

In a similar spirit, the odd antique or salvaged piece of furniture can work happily side by side with modern furnishings. Utility fittings and furniture have an in-built compatibility, but even finer decorative pieces, such as antique gilded mirrors or carved wooden chests, can make sympathetic additions.

Above **White on white is always successful as long as the palette is not taken to extremes. Here, subtle tones of barely off-white work together on and around a maple floor. Rustic wooden chairs have been given a contemporary facelift with a coat of paint.**

SOFT FURNISHINGS

Gone are the days when modernity meant uncompromising right angles, hard surfaces and the comfort levels of the average monk's cell. Simplicity and clarity of design are not incompatible with the pleasures of life, and soft furnishings – cushions, throws and upholstered covers – can provide a layer of warmth and comfort that is important to more than just our physical well-being.

Loose covers are supremely practical for sofas and easy chairs, and many contemporary pieces are available with this option. Loose

Right **A classic Chesterfield sofa upholstered in mock cowhide is a tongue-in-cheek statement in an otherwise industrial kitchen area, creating instant glamour and warmth.**

Below **Chunky, cube-like storage units, which discreetly house hi-fi equipment and a large music collection, also act as a room-divider and a frame for the contemporary sofa.**

covers need not be the pleated, skirted affairs typically found in chintzy drawing rooms; Velcro fastenings enable a tight, tailored fit that reveals the basic shape of the piece. Strong indigo blues, deep red, mustard and grass green provide solid blocks of colour for a graphic accent. Alternatively, for a look of cool sophistication, try white.

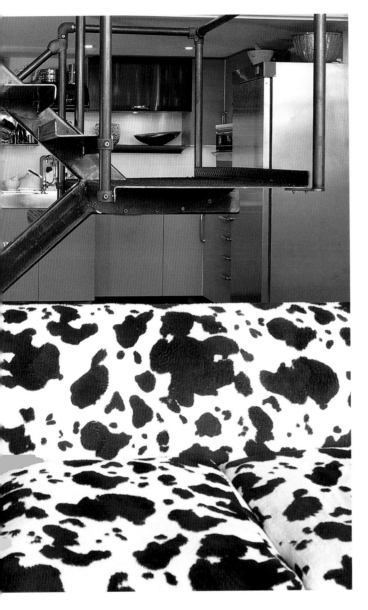

Upholstery tends to wear out well in advance of the basic framework but recovering can be expensive. For a cheap and cheerful coverup, you can transform a sofa that has some life left in it with quilted, tailored or waffle weave throws in off-white or a solid shade. Soft woollen blankets in moody neutrals or fake fur rugs may be a welcome addition on a chilly night.

Cushions soften the lines of clean-cut modern furniture and offer the opportunity to ring the changes with colour and texture, as well as shape. Fake fur fabric has great tongue-in-cheek potential; inflatable see-through cushions are a must for devotees of Pop, while one designer has brought out a range of brightly coloured round seat cushions in neoprene.

Above **This unadorned but inviting fireplace demands to be a focal point, so richly textured floor cushions have been placed enticingly near. Candles and elegant, frosted bottles holding single stems complete the sensory experience.**

Above **Wood and stainless steel fittings sit well against these walls of luscious apple green and lavender. A glass-topped table capitalizes on the light streaming in through the skylight and offers an additional reflective surface.**

FIXTURES AND FITTINGS

Contemporary decorating brings colour and texture to the order and efficiency of the modern interior, and different materials for built-in fixtures and fittings provide an ideal way of introducing variety and character. The kitchen is one area in the home where modernism has often seemed most natural and expected. Kitchens are first and foremost workplaces, where appliances and services must be well integrated in a seamless, logical fashion. But, increasingly, kitchens are where many of us spend much of our time at home, engaged in all kinds of activities only tangentially related to cooking. The kitchen, as a living space, needs to be as soulful as the rest of the home.

In a kitchen, the worktop is a natural site for material expression: solid slabs or planes of granite, wood, metal and laminate contrast effectively with discreet fitted units. Splashbacks in zinc, tile or security glass have a sleek, hard-edged aesthetic.

If you cannot afford to rip out an old kitchen and start from scratch, basic units, drawers or cupboards can be upgraded quite simply and economically. Paint will cover a multitude of sins, and it is even possible to paint over kitchen tiling that you do not like. New door or drawer fronts can be constructed and installed by a carpenter: razor-sharp flush panels or glazed doors can be substituted for old fielded or moulded fronts and accessorized with new handles.

While the fitted kitchen was once the height of modernity, the contemporary look can now be readily achieved with free-standing unfitted kitchen storage pieces – a good solution if you want to take your investment with you when you move. Butcher's block tables, and modern versions of classic storage furniture such as dressers, are now available in designs that do not automatically evoke the below-stairs life of yesteryear. Alternatively, secondhand shops can be a good source of painted or metal 'maid-servers', commonplace all-in-one kitchen

Left **A mixture of fixed and free-standing units is the contemporary answer to the dull, homogenous fitted kitchen look. A wine rack has been incorporated into a unit that fits around a free-standing refrigerator and gleaming panelled cupboard.**

Below **Ready to move at a moment's notice, hardboard-faced units on industrial casters are individually stylish. Finished off with thick beech worktops and extendable halogen ceiling spots, they are exciting alternatives to mass-manufactured systems.**

cabinets from the prewar era. Taking the unfitted idea to its logical conclusion, plug-in, fully serviced kitchen 'workbenches' that incorporate stove, sink and worksurface in one movable design are also available.

As our palates grow more sophisticated and culinary horizons broaden, one obvious point of reference – and inspiration – is the professional kitchen. The paraphernalia of serious cooking – utensils, equipment and cooking pots of all kinds – make a working display on wall-mounted racks or hanging rails. In a similar vein, catering-size appliances in gleaming steel are increasingly popular on the domestic scene. Huge metal fridges with see-through glass doors make a dramatic addition to the kitchen. For a more irreverent look, fridges are now available in brilliant shocking colours – or you could even paint an old fridge yourself.

Another essentially fitted room, the bathroom is a place of renewal, where the tensions of the day can be soaked away in warm, scented water. Contemporary decorating focuses on these elemental qualities to create a restorative haven for the senses.

Of all the areas in the home, the bathroom lacks a significant history. Indoor plumbing came late in the development of the domestic house and for many decades the decorative and design potential of the bathroom was all but ignored. That situation has changed radically in recent years, with a wealth of innovative designs for bathroom fittings and fixtures coming onto the market. Shaped and sunken baths, capsule-like shower cubicles, basins that sit like glass bowls on a tabletop, and graphic taps (faucets) and levers are at the forefront of modern bathroom design. While traditional fittings preserve the Edwardian solidity of the first mass-market sanitaryware, these new versions take inspiration from more basic sources, such as Japanese hot tubs. Buckets and wooden wash tubs were among the reference points for Philippe Starck's original bathroom fixtures.

In some contemporary designs, plumbing is not hidden away: basins inset in free-standing consoles are drained by visible and sculptural pipework. At the opposite extreme, the fitting of fixtures can be so well integrated that the room reads as a seamless whole.

If you cannot afford to invest in a brand-new bathroom suite, you can give standard fittings a fresh, modern look with handsome modern accessories: gleaming chrome taps,

burnished metal cosmetic cabinets, concertina-arm shaving mirrors, heated towel rails and free-standing metal and glass shelving.

In the contemporary interior, humble fixtures such as radiators can be dramatically expressive elements. The standard panel radiator occupies a significant amount of wall space, restricting options for furniture arrangement; and no one could claim that it makes an interesting feature in its own right. However, modern radiator designs are far from mundane. Long low coils hug the perimeter of a room at base line, while wall-hung springs and grids introduce a lively graphic note. Alternatively, retro-style radiators in bright colours are available for a strong sense of character.

Above **Chrome bathroom fittings are a significant detail in a modern scheme. An enormous range of sculptural designs is available on the market.**

Left **Fitted with hanging rails, this chrome radiator doubles as a towel rack, thereby saving space and energy and ensuring that a shower cubicle as well as a shallow bathing area will fit into this narrow space.**

Far left **More artform than washbasin, this handmade glass bowl carries water down through a glass funnel into the plumbing system – a true meeting of traditional craftsmanship and modern technology.**

Right **A retro glass-topped table and floor lamp prove that furniture need not be new to be contemporary, although many designers today are drawing on the shapes and forms in vogue 40 years ago for their inspiration.**

Above **The sleek, long lines of chrome handles on wooden storage units provide a strong graphic edge.**

DETAILS

Extending the contemporary look to the details and incidental fittings of your home provides an easy and economical transformation. Metal light switches and socket covers, sleek modern door handles in chrome, bright resin knobs for drawers – all provide an instant uplift. On flush panel doors or plain fitted units, such details provide a flourish of interest that makes the entire effect look carefully considered as well as twice as expensive.

Essential but everyday items such as wastepaper baskets and laundry bins can be dull and unlovely – or they can add a more positive note to your surroundings. Plastic, which not so long ago was reviled as a cheap, unpleasant and unfriendly material, has undergone something of a renaissance in recent years. New developments in plastics technology have given rise to a form of polypropylene that is subtly textured and translucent and can be dyed in brilliant shades. New plastic bins and containers, with their smooth moulded forms and luminous colours, are no longer second-best. Plywood is another material that has seen a revival and is now used to fashion elegant home accessories, from magazine racks to slot-together wastepaper baskets. Metal containers of all descriptions are another option, while for simple, cheap utility, try wire mesh baskets.

LIGHTING

Light is the partner of shadow, revealing texture, describing volume, enclosing and defining space. Natural sources, such as firelight, sunlight and candlelight, have innate variety, a fluctuation of direction, intensity and level that is instinctively appealing. Contemporary lighting seeks to emulate the vitality of natural light, to bring sparkle and drama to the home.

All too often, artificial light is seen merely as a practical means of providing enough illumination to work or see by once night has fallen. Lighting a room with a few, bright overhead fixtures may well serve your purpose, but it is also the surest way to deaden atmosphere. No matter how much effort and expense it may have taken to decorate and furnish a room, poor or unimaginative lighting is the design equivalent of a passion-killer. Conversely, good lighting gives instant uplift and can make even mundane surroundings a little magical.

How and where to light are decisions that should take precedence over the style or appearance of the light itself. Once you have planned a scheme, you can think about choosing a lamp or fitting: acquiring lights in a piecemeal fashion, seduced into purchase by the way they look, will never result in an atmospheric or even practical effect.

All rooms or areas need a variety of light sources to provide general or background illumination, concentrated work or task lighting and moody or decorative accent light. Most people overlight their rooms, but have too few light sources. As a rough rule of thumb, plan to

Below **A renewed enthusiasm for plywood has led to birch ply veneer being used on a variety of contemporary accessories, from wastepaper baskets to fruit bowls. It is also well suited to lampshades, its pliability and translucence creating an atmospheric glow.**

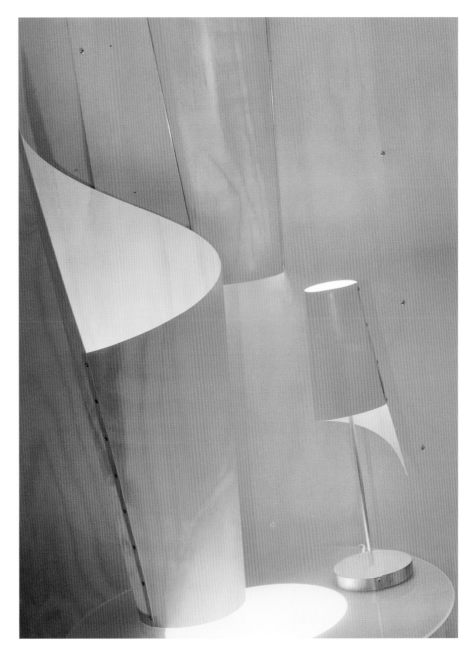

Right **A low-voltage barewire installation is the ultimate minimal lighting system. Tensioned cables carry the charge and are used as a supporting framework for small low-voltage lights, which can be positioned anywhere along the network. A wall-mounted uplighter provides discreet ambient lighting.**

include no fewer than five different lights in the average-sized living room – individually these need not be very bright, but together they will create overlapping pools of light and shade to provide definition and vitality.

For background lighting, use the ceiling as a reflector and direct light upwards. Light bounced off the ceiling creates a soothing level of illumination without glare. A similar effect can be gained with wall-mounted sconces or wall-washers that bathe the upper parts of the room in a soft glow. By contrast, bright, central pendant fixtures cast light evenly in all directions, which can be tiring and oppressive.

Individual table lamps create warm, cosy focal points around the room. These can be wired centrally to a main switch by the door and controlled by a dimmer to provide instant changes of atmosphere and mood.

Concentrated light is needed wherever there is work to do. Task lights, such as the classic Anglepoise, give a focused beam to light a page. Ceiling-mounted spotlights and down-lights are good for kitchen surfaces.

Until fairly recently, domestic lighting relied almost entirely on tungsten bulbs – with the odd hideously green-tinged fluorescent strip thrown in for utility purposes. Tungsten has much to recommend it as a light source for the home, since it produces a warm, yellowish cast that is soft on the eyes and flattering to the complexion. But light sources today also include halogen, which was formerly restricted to retail lighting. Halogen bulbs are small, which means fittings can be discreet, and produce a bright,

sparkling light that is very true to colours. In contemporary interiors, where pure white meets planes of brilliant shades, halogen can be a good partner for decoration.

Lighting is one of the most vibrant and exciting fields of modern design and the range available is spectacular – everything from minimal recessed fittings that twinkle in the ceiling like stars to exuberant and expressive lamps in innovative materials. The 'designer' lights of the previous decade, typified by such prototypes as the angular matt black Tizio, have given way to more sculptural and playful styles. Lighting as 'software' rather than 'hardware' concentrates on the different effects that can be achieved with shading – using envelopes of ply, woven silk, extruded resin and corrugated paper to make spirals, cones and sculptural folds. Even the standard paper globe shade, that anonymous lighting stopgap, has re-emerged in a variety of organic shapes to create a Brancusi-like effect.

Borrowing from both the industrial and commercial worlds, there are over-scale photographer's lights, aluminium and spun-metal pendants and simple clip-on spots. Large lofty spaces may be lit by barewire installation, whereby individual halogen spots are suspended from a visible trapeze-like network of cabling. Track lights have been transformed from obvious spots on cumbersome ceiling-mounted runners to spare and elegant fittings fixed to narrow parallel rails.

Table lamps have also undergone a makeover. A wry, low-tech solution is offered by British designer Michael Marriott's self-assembly wire stand where the lightbulb is shaded by the postcard of your choice. Philippe Starck's instantly recognizable all-in-one table lamp, Miss Sissi, made out of moulded plastic, has given a contemporary twist to a traditional form. Jewelled or wire-shaded lights that light up only themselves – not the surrounding area – make decorative accents. More architecturally, low lights set in skirtings (baseboards) or flanking the stairs have unbeatable drama.

Above **Clip-on loft lights provide versatile accent lighting. The matt metal shades have a suitably architectural edge to go with the heavy-duty metal shelving. Trailing wires are all part of the no-nonsense aesthetic.**

Left **Svelte and witty, this fake-fur table lamp on tall wire legs brings an element of humour and irreverence to a cool, classic interior.**

Textured cushions

These simple cushions disprove the notion that contemporary decorating is all about hard edges and monochrome: here you have comfort, colour and interesting texture rolled into one. Favourite sweaters that no longer fit, suede offcuts, and even redundant sheepskin rugs can all be re-cycled to make cushion covers. Other materials you can use include raffia matting, leather, hessian (burlap) and upholstery webbing.

When working with suede, experiment on an offcut first so you can get used to how the fabric handles. Although suede is tough, it marks easily, so make sure any pin marks will not show on the right side of the fabric.

MATERIALS AND TOOLS

• Hand-knitted sweater • Suede offcut • Sheepskin offcut • Sewing machine and thread • Cushion pads • Scissors • Razor blade or sharp scalpel (craft knife) • Straightedge or steel rule • Fabric marker pen

METHOD

1 For the sweater cushion cover: Cut off the arms of the sweater with scissors. Turn the sweater inside out (i.e., right sides facing) and machine-hem the bottom, ribbed edge of the sweater, leaving a big enough gap in the middle for inserting the cushion pad. Pin 12mm (½ in) in from the neck line to give the top of the cover a straight edge. Do the same for the cut side seams. Machine-hem the side and top seams. Turn the sweater the right way round and insert the cushion pad. Oversew the gap in the bottom edge by hand.

2 For the sheepskin cover: On the back of the skin, and using the marker pen, mark out two squares, each the same size as the cushion pad, adding an extra 12mm (½in) all round for the seams. Cut the skin with a sharp scalpel (craft knife) or razor blade, pulling the cut skin tightly away from you as you go. Do not use scissors as they will crop the pile.

Pin and machine-sew the pieces together, 12mm (½in) in from the edges, leaving a gap in the fourth side for the cushion pad. Clip all four corners of the skin diagonally, about 6mm (¼in) away from the stitching, so when the cover is turned the right way, the corners are less bundled. Turn the cover the right way out, insert the cushion pad and oversew the gap.

3 For the suede cover: Cut the fabric to size, as for the sheepskin cover, making sure you draw the lines lightly on the smooth side of the suede to avoid stretching and press firmly on the straightedge. Place the two squares right sides facing and pin together carefully. Machine-sew the squares together, 12mm (½in) in from the edge, to make a flat seam. Leave an opening in one side for the pad.

To make a double topstitched seam for a decorative finish (see photograph), press open the flat seams and topstitch each seam allowance to the main fabric. The lines of top-stitching should be about 6mm (¼in) from the seam line. On the fourth side, where the pad is inserted, close up the gap by hand-sewing.

Revamped tabletop

A badly scratched table can be restored and given a contemporary look by applying a couple of coats of paint to a sheet of Perspex (Plexiglas) and fixing it over the existing tabletop with metal corner brackets.

This small, black-painted and rather worn table has been transformed into a sleek, white kitchen table, perfect for the modern home. The same method can also be applied to small bedside tables and large, low coffee tables. You can also try sandwiching flat objects, such as leaves, postcards, photographs, cut-out cardboard or paper shapes or reflective paper, between the tabletop and a sheet of unpainted Perspex. It is a good idea to glue the objects to the tabletop to stop them moving when you lay the Perspex on top.

Perspex is available from plastics suppliers who will cut it to your exact measurements. If you are prepared to pay a little more, you could ask for Perspex with a polished edge. The smoother finish is kinder to the touch and does not show any saw marks.

MATERIALS AND TOOLS

• Sheet of Perspex (Plexiglas) • Paint kettle
• Sandpaper • Matt white emulsion paint
• 10cm (4in) paintbrush or roller • 4 metal table corner brackets • Hammer • Panel pins (brads)

METHOD

1 Apply a coat of white matt emulsion paint with a brush or roller to one side of the pre-cut Perspex (Plexiglas) sheeting. Allow to dry.

2 If your table is in poor condition, you will need to sand it down (leave the tabletop) to remove any excess paint or varnish. If the layers are thick, use paint or varnish stripper first.

Apply two coats of matt white emulsion to the table, again omitting the tabletop, allowing the paint to dry after each coat. Once dry, lay the sheet of Perspex, painted side down, on top of the table. Attach metal brackets to each corner in turn, using a hammer and panel pins (brads) to secure in position.

STORAGE & DISPLAY

STORAGE & DISPLAY

New moderns revel in discreet display as a means of softening the hard edges of contemporary design. Display, in the contemporary sense of the word, is the antithesis of untidy and overcrowded shelves that spill knick-knacks in a ramshackle fashion. It is much more about honed style – the showing of simple, dramatic objects, whether by size, texture, colour or form. It is also about introducing your own personality into the living space.

In a contemporary scheme, where walls and windows, floors and fittings merge together effortlessly in a soothing cohesion, display focuses the eye. The danger in modern rooms is that they can sometimes look too calculated, and it is often the display details that provide much-needed softness and individuality. Whether it is an enormous urn containing over-sized branches and twigs, a plain glass vase filled with bold blooms or dense green foliage, a striking painting or strong sculptural form, these personal statements lend wit and colour to spaces where clutter has been completely banished from view.

As clean lines and a sense of calm are key elements of contemporary decorating, the objects with which you choose to decorate your space should be able to work on their own merits, as graphic counterpoints to the rest of the room. In a sparsely styled room, the furniture itself can become a valuable display item. A jewel-bright sofa dressed with cushions covered in nubbly wool, textured velvet or eye-catching fake fur makes a strong statement in its own right, while a well-lit display of textured

stoneware set on a simple wooden sideboard against a white wall is exquisite to behold. Provided they are chosen with care, everyday items, such as bowls, teapots, bottles or baskets, will all withstand scrutiny in a pared-down room. Simple is often serene.

MIXING OLD WITH NEW

The most successful contemporary interiors are often, ironically, born of an old building that has been stripped of its inner divisions and reinterpreted. Those who have opted for lofts, warehouses and other industrial buildings have found a way of living with the past without adopting an outmoded and nostalgic lifestyle. Nowadays, homes have evolved so that simplicity and convenience are central to the ethos of contemporary living. The functions of cooking and eating, working and relaxing flow into one another and co-exist quite happily. Living rooms are multi-functional spaces rather than formal drawing rooms. Therefore, a room stuffed with elaborate antique furniture that was designed for a specific use, or with artefacts from a bygone age, can now seem completely irrelevant in this age of practicality and economy. However, a single, beautiful armoire for storing modern paraphernalia such as video tapes, compact discs and computer monitors can sit in happy juxtaposition with cool glass shelving or post-Modern ceramics. Similarly, a beautiful 1930s vase of white lilies is both retro and modern. Mixing and matching the old with the new can look utterly contemporary while providing practical design solutions.

Above **A quixotic mix of design classics and disparate objects works as decorative relief in this bare-walled and dark-floored converted industrial building.**

Left **A large abstract artwork provides a softening effect against pale walls and the neutral-coloured sofa. A coffee table, created from a piece of hewn slate, an underbelly of light timber and strong industrial casters, is both elegant and functional.**

Above **This fireplace has been stripped of its decorative and functional elements and reinterpreted with paint as discreet architectural punctuation and display space. The floorboards have been extended into the hearth for a sense of continuity.**

PARING DOWN

In some ways, contemporary display is more about what you hide away than what you accentuate or pinpoint. Creating a strong, uncluttered display should start with a paring down of your possessions, if the modern mantra of space, light and versatility is to work well.

Begin with the mantelpiece, if you have one. This is the one place in a room where people reveal their signature, whether it be grainy photographs, carefully chosen ceramics or a statement vase of flowers. Take away all ornament until you have a clear surface with which to start again. Then judge each decorative object on its own merits. Does it add colour, texture or spiritual warmth? If a treasured photograph elicits an emotional response but sits in a heavy gilt frame more suited to a country

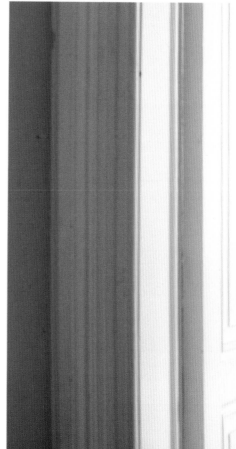

home, then change the frame, or even slip the photo between two pieces of clear Perspex (Plexiglas). Strip away the ornamentation and you still have your important belongings around you – clean and calm, simple and soulful.

Take a critical look, too, at all your shelves and dressers, occasional tables and walls. Are there too many pictures and possessions fighting for attention so that they present a muddled vista when you walk into a room? Banish objects that no longer give you pleasure, or look rather tired, to the attic or a garage sale. Or simply give your belongings a rest in a cupboard or shed until you want to see them again.

PUTTING AWAY

Once you have pared down the contents of your living space, there will inevitably be 'stuff' left over that demands to be stored. Very often, bright boxes on pigeon-hole shelves or small wooden containers on glass shelves will provide both effective storage and eye-catching display at the same time. Hiding away whatever is superfluous does demand a certain degree of tidiness, but this is easily achieved if you incorporate enough 'slinging places' for those irritating pieces of paper, chewed toys and redundant plastic shopping bags that often clutter the home.

You can never really have enough integral or free-standing cupboards or large pieces of furniture that provide storage caches. Large boxes on casters, oversized baskets and generous cupboards or shelving systems in each room will help you to maintain a sense of space as well as create clean lines.

Above **Strong and elegant in their own right, these narrow, floor-to-ceiling cupboards are further enhanced with tiny, metal door catches, lightweight chicken wire and uniform cardboard boxes. Catalogued with numbers, the boxes hide all sorts of ugly clutter.**

Left **This pared-down display of a giant seed pod and abstract painting leaning against the wall assumes graphic definition alongside a rough slate shelf, polished wood floorboards and brown, textural chairs.**

Right Sliding doors in ribbed plastic provide intriguing silhouettes of the contents of this cupboard. Small Perspex (Plexiglas) knobs at each shelf level lend pleasing symmetry to the finished cabinet.

Far right A discreet plasterboard divider has been built around a steel support girder as the anchor for clothes storage and mock wall for plywood storage drawers. In this converted loft space, storage and display are one and the same.

Below No space is wasted in this custom-built staircase that incorporates deep, pull-out drawers for storing anything from cans of food to boots and shoes.

SHELVES, DRAWERS AND CUPBOARDS

Alcoves are good places for both storage and display. Built-in shelves edged with a thick lip of plywood, MDF (particleboard) or hardwood which is then painted the same colour as the walls will merge the two spaces together and provide graphic definition for whatever you place there – a pleasing collection of oversized books, striking ceramic bowls or a combination of sculpture, flowers and small photographs. For a minimalist feel, install simple glass shelves resting on thin metal supports driven into the wall, or mount them 'invisibly' with Perspex (Plexiglas) supports. Alternatively, suspend them with tension wire from the wall or ceiling. Such elegant constructions demand aesthetic objects to set them off, while tiny halogen downlighters will add sparkling definition to the display. Curvaceous shelves can be created by bending steel sheeting or moulding plywood to form organic shapes against a wall.

Drawers are important vessels for storage in modern interiors. They can be incorporated seamlessly into the structure of a room in alcoves, under staircases or even under individual stairs. The idea of low platform-cum-seating is a versatile one: deep wooden drawers pull out from underneath a seat to reveal video tapes, blankets, toys or paperwork.

Wall-mounted cupboards or sets of shelves can become contemporary display pieces, too. Make or finish them with interesting materials, such as zinc cladding punctuated with galvanized nails, glass-fronted doors with coloured glass knobs, or alternate strips of corrugated plastic and plywood or beech. Cupboard doors can be left open or ajar occasionally to reveal the contents within – an element of surprise is always appealing. Mirrored cabinets placed opposite a wall of strong colour or a dynamic painting will enlarge the space and reflect colour and definition back into a room.

The industrial-style kitchen, long favoured by architects, has permeated through to general acceptance, with stainless steel appliances, utensils and metal worktops and cupboards becoming increasingly popular. Open metal shelving systems are simple, functional items. Using them for storage often begets an effortless display,

allowing you to both store and show pleasing collections of white china, table linen, stainless steel kitchenware and colourful cans of food.

Clothes storage has for too long been consigned to period-style free-standing cupboards. Contemporary cupboards are streamlined, seamless and eminently practical. Folding doors in plywood or MDF (particleboard), beech or birch are simply hinged to open with a gentle push, or else door furniture is pure and understated. Free-standing clothes storage in the form of an 'open-plan' wardrobe is also an option. Tall-sided warehouse trolleys on casters

can be fitted with shelves for storing boxes of sweaters, shirts and underwear. Clothes rails are the ultimate in function, while ordinary wardrobes can be revamped with glass-fronted doors and casters for flexibility.

The sideboard has escaped from the now defunct dining room and new interpretations can be found in the living room, kitchen and bedroom. Basically storage units on legs or wheels, the new streamlined versions range from the strictly rectangular to curved plywood, also employing materials such as Formica, birch ply and aluminium.

MOBILE STORAGE

Casters are contemporary decorating's answer to the stripped pine of the 1970s. No serious modernist would be without their wheels. In the living room, casters fixed to furniture, home entertainment units, sliding screens or simple storage boxes allow great freedom with your layout, enabling you to rearrange furniture and take storage receptacles with you around the room, according to your needs.

In the kitchen, bathroom and bedroom, plastic stacking boxes on wheels are heaven-sent for containing clutter. In the bedroom, they can be filled with unsightly shoes and papers and then wheeled out of sight behind a discreet screen (also on casters). Use them as a display in the bathroom, piled with matching toiletry bottles or metal boxes. Similarly, a metal trolley on casters can make a virtue of a colourful towel collection. Toy trunks in plywood with rope handles, casters and brakes are a real treasure, making instant tidy-ups a distinct possibility.

Even beds can benefit from a set of wheels. A few strictly minimal architects have been known to use redundant hospital beds as the basis for their bedroom scheme. While subtler variations of this approach are probably more appealing, a bed on wheels does allow you to move it easily for cleaning and to get at any under-bed storage quickly.

REUSING MATERIALS

Shop, school, kitchen and office fittings, either classic or contemporary, all fit well into a modern setting. The humble metal filing cabinet

Above **Tea chests have been strapped together with luggage belts, separated with blocks of wood and faced with tin for a stylish, whimsical but thoroughly economical take on a chest of drawers.**

Left **Industrial casters fixed to the bottom of an aluminium trunk provide a shiny, movable feast in a spare loft living space.**

has been appropriated by many for its sleek, colourful functionalism. Sprayed silver or painted in vivid colours, its classic proportions also make it suitable for use as an occasional table, under-table storage or even a long, low storage bench, if several are gathered together under a window.

Schools have yielded metal mesh clothes and shoe lockers, which can be as narrow or wide as you like – perfect for filling an alcove in a child's or teenager's room, or as a stylish unbroken run in a bedroom. Refectory tables that have deep storage drawers built into them provide a warm and weathered antidote to care-fully considered super-modern dining chairs, as well as effective storage.

Shop fittings such as glass-fronted drapers' drawers or wooden display cabinets also make a virtue of both storage and display.

Above **Pieces of reclaimed wood have been transformed into a filing cabinet, softening the ultra-contemporary tabletop and chair alongside. Drawers with discreet metal handles pull open to reveal well-organized spaces within.**

PLAYING WITH SCALE

Creating a sense of space is important in contemporary decorating and can be achieved through colour, materials and display. However, even an all-white room punctuated with blond wood furniture and fittings can start to feel claustrophobic if it is littered with too many keepsakes and photographic trophies from every era of your life.

Many contemporary schemes rely on a sense of symmetry to create their impact, so it is invigorating to break the pattern from time to time. On a bedroom or living room wall, place a picture just above the bed or sofa at one corner. It will draw the eye towards it and produce a pleasingly skewed perspective.

To open up the space in a tiny room, use a few carefully placed, oversized objects to give the impression of a grander room. A bold sofa flanked by a huge stone urn filled with tall twigs or blooms is simple, chic and economic with the space. Why clog a small wall with miniature prints when a single huge painting will provide drama and an interesting contrast in scale?

MINIMAL DISPLAY

The antithesis of cluttered walls and shelves is nowhere more apparent than in Japan, where interiors continue to exert a strong influence on many contemporary designers in the West. Japanese rooms, often scrupulously bare save for one or two dramatically placed items, are almost anti-display. Yet this strictly minimal approach to showing objects can work very well. Whether flowers or art, wallhanging or propped object, experiment with the grand, one-off statement. Such a simple showpiece is, of course, easy to swap for something else in the Japanese tradition of rotating display, so its impact can be renewed regularly. This approach also allows emphasis to be placed on the structural elements of a room – walls, floor and ceiling – and on natural light.

Far left **An arrangement of miniature wall-mounted cupboards is both a graphic display and a network of storage units.**

Left **A large, pale canvas, small cushions, a wafer-thin table positioned against intriguing screen doors and a huge urn of contorted twigs are all the ostentation needed in this serene space.**

Right **Kitsch and pink seem made for each other, although complete overkill has been averted here with the smoked-glass tabletop and simple black and white floor tiles. A touch of turquoise from the chair and vase echoes the retro sideboard.**

Below **A comprehensive collection of 1950s ceramics makes a graphic display on black lacquered shelving. The design of this period, as displayed in textiles, ceramics and furnishings, retains a refreshing modernity of form and pattern which brings character to contemporary decorating.**

INTRODUCING HUMOUR

In the 1960s, when popular culture permeated homes as thoroughly as it did music, fashion and graphics, kitsch was king. Lurid lava lamps, primary-coloured inflatable furniture, and wobbly, woozy fabric designs were the must-haves of the day. Some of the less ridiculous elements of the style have enjoyed a resurgence, among them the crisp colour schemes of chocolate and cream, orange and lime. Meanwhile, lava lamps and 1960s ceramics are achieving respectable prices at auction and the coloured glass vases, bowls and sculptures that were once the preserve of every rented apartment have become covetable. Used prudently, a touch of kitsch provides a sense of humour and a discreet nod to the modernizing influence of the pop decade.

PRIMITIVE STYLE

Ethnic artefacts are often found in strikingly modern surroundings. They provide a real sense of history and tradition and exhibit a respect for the past and the handmade aesthetic which contrasts pleasingly with new forms of decorating and architecture.

Bold, naive prints in brown and biscuit and African carvings can provide an international flavour, as well as juxtaposing old with new, primitive with machine-made, in today's home.

Ethnic textiles, too, often complement modern schemes. Striking geometric motifs and nubbly stripes sit happily with planes of solid colour and contrast well with an all-white scheme. Similarly, wall hangings of woven wool, interlocking fabric or naive appliqué make soft contrasts with the harder materials inherent in modern design. Wood and metal sculptures, rough-coiled pottery and clay objects also provide a counterpoint to the smooth, sleek lines of contemporary rooms.

Above **Carved African gourds, a woven basket and sculptured head against a backdrop of lilac feathers give this display a strong cultural character.**

Left **These curvy wall shelves have become instant design classics; their display and storage potential, as well as their sense of fun, is immediately appealing. Together, the shelves and the contemporary lime green sofa provide ample decorative interest.**

Right **Simple whitewashed walls and fireplace are home to a quirky sculpture, pebble and single tulip: an exercise in creating interest with contrasting textures and materials.**

HANDCRAFTED ORIGINALS

The notion of handcrafted objects in a contemporary interior may seem surprising, but it is curiously relevant. Handmade one-off pieces of furniture, ceramics or works of art dilute the discipline of modernist principles, providing a touch of the artisan and a welcome informality.

The new craftspeople are experimenting with a wide range of different materials, such as concrete, moulded plastic fibres and metal, to create tomorrow's classics. Just as the Arts and Crafts Movement of the early 1900s was born of a frustration with the mass-produced industrial aesthetic, so today's contemporary craftspeople are enjoying patronage from leading architects and designers as a means of introducing individual identity and personality into modern homes.

NATURAL DISPLAYS

Generously filled containers of natural flowers and foliage are pleasing additions to a modern interior. Simple glass or plain ceramic vases work best. Fill them with contorted willow branches, bird of paradise flowers, white stocks or vibrant gerberas. These signature flowers and foliage are as familiar in contemporary decorating as the aspidistra plant was to the Victorians, and they are perfect foils for the simplicity of modern living.

Colourful and richly textured foliage will add zing to any room. An abundant display of grey-green eucalyptus, yellow forsythia or tall, sapphire-coloured delphiniums make for exhilarating contrasts of colour. In an all-white scheme, a dramatic display of yellow, red or orange flowers can accentuate colour details in soft furnishings, such as cushions, rugs and window treatments, or pick out details in a painting or other work of art.

Everyday containers are good foils to the formality of sculptural flowers and greenery favoured by contemporary decorators. Galvanized buckets, empty milk bottles or unpretentious laboratory bottles and test tubes can all be put to use. Industrial kitchen accessories have also been appropriated by contemporary decorators. Wire fruit and egg baskets, catering-size steel trays and caskets all make suitable receptacles for collected possessions, whether they are postcards, pine cones, table linen or papers.

Branches of gnarled driftwood, balls of lava stone and smooth, patterned pebbles, or pure pieces such as plastercast images resting on

white surfaces, all lend an earthy and uncomplicated feel to highly structured spaces. Many architects deliberately include an element of nature in their tautly devised contemporary interiors: slim tree trunks may be used as softening columns in a room, or blond wood beams may be inserted above a doorway as a visual reference to nature.

Above **Delicate vases resembling test tubes are perfect containers for single stems of vivid red gerberas, the ultimate contemporary flowers with their graphic shape and bold colour.**

Left **Striped and textured pebbles stashed in a simple bowl bring nature to an unadorned window sill. Hints of blue are found in both the window glazing and pottery.**

SENSUOUS DISPLAYS

Scent is an integral part of your home and an important sensory device for providing tranquillity and atmosphere. Perfumed flowers can be supplemented with scented candles of eucalyptus, sandalwood or lemon, pots of fresh herbs and herb-scented pot-pourri and incense. In kitchens and bathrooms, choose soap with an enriching perfume such as citrus fruit. For the combination of scent and flickering light, fill deep glass bowls with water and crown them with floating scented candles to provide restorative sparkle and a sensory treat.

As a pleasing contrast to the clean lines of modern living, candles enjoy an elevated status in many contemporary homes. Especially fashionable for large living areas are huge geometric candles with multiple wicks. These richly textured Turkish candles are at once heat source, furniture, decorative object and sensory reinforcer. Candles in numbers – a small, heatproof tray filled with ten or more nightlights and placed on a draught-free, level surface, for example – are particularly special. Or line up chunky butter-coloured candles in a variety of sizes on a mantelpiece for simple drama.

WALL DISPLAYS

Contemporary picture frames are usually understated: simple, narrow, painted or plain wooden frames – or no frame at all, just clipped glass or Perspex (Plexiglas) sheets pierced with metal fasteners. Sometimes an empty frame will be hung from a wall as a distinctive minimalist statement. If this is going too far, then consider other options. In modern surroundings, pencil and ink drawings work well, as do abstract prints and bold, colourful paintings. The art of propping, as pioneered by Donna Karan in her American home, has taken off in the smartest interiors. A few careworn mirrors or images in battered gilt frames are simply propped against a bare wall or immaculate skirting (baseboard) rather than hung on the wall.

Functionalism and flexibility are an important consideration in contemporary decorating. One way of displaying your favourite images so they can evolve or swap around is to create a noticeboard in a hallway or kitchen. Employ a casual approach to your chosen board, using postcards, fabric swatches or photocopied images to play down the formality of modern style and make the most of your ideas, shopping lists, messages, sketches and so on. An ultra-sleek alternative is a huge sheet of stainless steel, to which various images can be attached with round, black magnets. Or paint a sheet of plywood with blackboard paint and block off half a wall. White plastic boards and coloured markers, familiar from our days at school and college, would also work well in a strictly white room.

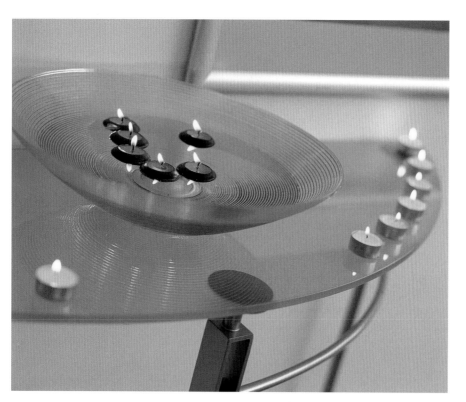

Above **Scented, coloured candles floating in a ribbed glass bowl and nightlights ranged round a circular table produce a peaceful, rippled light which dances on and around the glass surfaces to soften the surrounding hard edges.**

Laminated window hangings

One way of conserving and displaying treasured images is to have them covered in plastic laminate at a specialist laminators or photocopying shop. In this way you will be able to enjoy your pictures undistracted by an inappropriate frame.

We chose four, unmounted colour transparencies of close-ups of flowers and leaves and grouped them together at the window. Here the light appears to bounce through and around the images to create an eye-catching display, which is particularly colourful when the sun streams through the window.

Other ways of applying 'frameless' finishes include securing plastic sheets over your images with eyelets and hanging them with tension wire. For a more formal look, have your prints, posters or photographs mounted on board. They can then be laminated or left as they are.

MATERIALS AND TOOLS

• Colour transparencies, photographs or postcards • Cutting mat • Steel rule • Scalpel (craft knife) • Sheet of paper • Small bulldog clip • Transparent suction cup with hook

METHOD

On a tough surface, such as a cutting mat, and with the help of a steel rule, trim your favourite images with a sharp scalpel (craft knife). Arrange them in a square, rectangular or diamond configuration. Close cropping will give pictures extra emphasis, and white borders can be left on photographs for graphic definition.

Mark the position of the images in relation to each other on a sheet of paper as a guide for the laminator. Make sure that the edge of the laminate extends beyond the images so that nothing is obscured when the laminate is hung at the window.

The images can be hung in a number of ways. We attached a small bulldog clip to the laminate and hooked it over a suction cup which was stuck on the glass. You can also thread coloured string or wire through eyelets in the laminate (kits are available from hardware stores), and hang the images from a hook screwed into the window frame.

Veneer lampshade

Veneer, with its soft sheen, is easy on the eye, slightly translucent and pleasingly malleable, making it an ideal material for a lampshade. The sheet we used was magnolia veneer in an irregular rectangle, which allowed for a protruding edge at the top of the lamp.

As veneer is so thin, we recommend that you ask your veneer merchant or timber yard (lumberyard) to cut it to size for you. However, it is possible to do it yourself with a Stanley knife and steel straightedge on a cutting board. Be very gentle, though, as you work with such delicately thin strips of wood, and make sure you unroll them very carefully. You will find that the veneer curls naturally in one direction; do not force it to curl the opposite way. Too much pressure along the edges will cause it to tear.

We found a lamp base with a broken shade and wrapped the veneer into a freestanding tube over the existing fitting to create a floor lamp. Alternatively, you can buy a cheap lamp, discard the shade and create a simple, contemporary light source for the table.

Veneer, which is available in many different woods, and therefore in different colours, grains, weights and widths, can also be shaped to make distinctive shades for wall lights, not to mention lightweight bins and bowls.

MATERIALS

• Lamp base and light fitting • Sheet of magnolia veneer, cut to length • String • 5 x 5cm (2 x 2in) length of scrap wood • Stanley knife • Power drill and drill bit • Riveter and pop rivets • Washers

METHOD

1 Carefully fold one edge of the veneer over the other to form a cylinder, making sure that the top edge overlaps the bottom by approximately 8cm (3in). The easiest way to do this is to tie a number of pieces of string to the right circumference. Roll up the veneer too tightly and slip the pieces of string over it, allowing the veneer to expand into the constraining string to the correct size.

If you want a protruding upper edge to the lampshade, as here, the piece of veneer you use must be asymmetrical.

2 Slide left-over pieces of veneer under the string at intervals along the raw edge to prevent the string from cutting into the veneer. Push the batten through the cylinder and hang it over the backs of two chairs. This will support the veneer underneath as you drill. Drill holes every 10cm (4in) or so along the overlapped edge. Make sure you drill through both layers of veneer.

3 Stand the cylinder on a firm, flat surface. Rivet through both layers of veneer, and on the inside edge secure the rivets with washers. Cut a nick in the bottom edge for the flex (cord).

Mobile filing cabinet

Having shrugged off its utilitarian image, the workaday filing cabinet has become one of the classic storage solutions for the modern decorator. Its undisputed practicality and durability fit in with the new, no-nonsense approach to storage, which means that clutter is as undesirable as a dried flower arrangement; they both gather too much dust.

Casters fitted onto a filing cabinet will give added flexibility. Flexibility is the buzzword for furniture of the new millennium, and if it isn't multi-functional, it simply isn't modern.

If you do not want to go to the expense of buying a new filing cabinet, it is cheap and easy to give a second-hand one a contemporary look with a coat of paint.

Our painted 1970s version of classic proportions will look stylish in any room of the house. The heavy-duty casters we fitted for additional versatility are available from any good ironmongers or hardware store. Some types include brakes.

MATERIALS AND TOOLS

• Filing cabinet • Marker pen • Power drill and drill bit • Crosshead screwdriver or power screwdriver • 4 casters with self-tapping screws • Wet and dry sandpaper (grade 600 or 800) • Metal spray paint • Masking tape

METHOD

1 Remove the drawers from the filing cabinet and turn it upside down. Mark the position of the screws on the bottom of the cabinet by pushing a marker pen through each of the screw holes in the casters. Next, use a power drill to make fine holes. Screw the four casters in position with the crosshead screwdriver or power screwdriver.

2 Unscrew the handles on the drawers. Wash the surfaces of the filing cabinet and drawers with hot water and detergent to remove any dirt. To help the paint adhere to the surface, provide a key by rubbing back with wet and dry sandpaper. Allow to dry.

Cover any areas of the cabinet you do not want painted, such as the casters, with masking tape. Apply the spray paint according to the manufacturer's instructions. Leave to dry. Replace the handles and insert the drawers.

The ugly two-tone 'sophistication' of the late 1970s, when filing cabinets were invariably brown and cream, has given way to strong colours. Essential additions to the home office, up-to-date models are fashioned from aluminium. As well as the conventional two-drawer designs, there are also several shallow-drawer versions for storing and dividing paperwork. However, filing cabinets have now escaped the office environment as their practical application is fully appreciated. Increasingly, they are to be found in more unusual settings, as simple storage statements in pared-down living rooms, telephone tables in kitchens, toiletry storage units in bathrooms and television trolleys in teenagers' bedrooms.

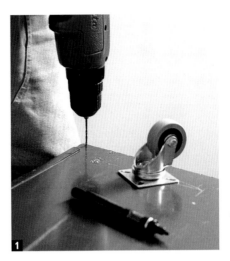

SOURCES

A selective list of suppliers of contemporary products.

Appliances

The American Appliance Centre, 19 Mill Lane, Woodford Green, Essex IG8 0UN
Tel: 020 8443 9999
• *American refrigerators and cooking ranges*

Robert Bosch Domestic Appliances, Grand Union House, Old Wolverton Road, Old Wolverton, Milton Keynes MK12 5PT
Tel: 01908 328200
• *full range of appliances, including 1950s-style refrigerators*

Siemens Domestic Appliances, *see under Robert Bosch for address*
Tel: 01908 328400
• *retro-style refrigerators in bright colours*

Radiators

Bisque Radiators Ltd, 244 Belsize Rd, London NW6 4BT
Tel: 020 7328 2225
• *designer radiators*

Clyde Combustions Ltd, Cox Lane, Chessington, Surrey KT9 1SL
Tel: 020 8391 2020

MHS Group, 35 Nobel Square, Burnt Mills Industrial Estate, Basildon, Essex SS13 1LT
Tel: 01268 591010

Radiating Style, Unit 15, Derby Road Industrial Estate, Derby Road, Hounslow, Middlesex TW3 3UH
Tel: 020 8577 9111

Ironmongery

Allgood Hardware, 297 Euston Road, London NW1 3AQ
Tel: 020 7387 9951
• *modern door furniture by designers such as Philippe Starck*

Franchi International, Unit 2/11 Chelsea Harbour Design Centre, Lots Road, London SW10 0XE
Tel: 020 7351 4554
• *modern architectural ironmongery*

Handles and Fittings Ltd, HAF House, Mead Lane, Hertford, Hertfordshire SG13 7AP
Tel: 01992 505655

Kee Klamp Ltd, 10 Worton Drive, Worton Grange, Reading, Berkshire RG2 0TQ
Tel: 0118 931 1022
• *high-tech, modular handrail systems*

Valli and Valli Ltd, 8 Gerard, Lichfield Road Industrial Estate, Tamworth, Staffordshire B79 7UW
Tel: 01827 63352
• *European door and furniture fittings, including designs by Sir Norman Foster*

Bathroom fittings

Aston-Matthews Ltd, 141-147a Essex Rd, London N1 2SN
Tel: 020 7226 7220

C P Hart, Newnham Terrace, Hercules Road, London SE1 7DR
Tel: 020 7902 1000

Original Bathrooms Ltd, 143-145 Kew Road, Richmond, Surrey TW9 2PN
Tel: 020 8940 7554

Kitchens

Bulthaup, 37 Wigmore Street, London W1H 9LD
Tel: 020 7495 3663

Crabtree Kitchens, The Sorting Office, 17 Station Road, Barnes, London SW13 0LF
Tel: 020 8392 6955

Fulham Kitchens, 19 Carnwath Road, London SW6 3HR
Tel: 020 7731 5166

Miele Co Ltd, Fairacres, Marcham Road, Abingdon, Oxfordshire OX14 1TW
Tel: 01235 554455

Lighting

Ambience, Alexandra House, Alexandra Terrace, Guildford, Surrey GU1 3DA
Tel: 01483 306601

Anglepoise Ltd, Unit 51, Enfield Industrial Area, Redditch, Worcestershire B97 6DR
Tel: 01527 63771

Aram Designs Ltd, 3 Kean Street, London WC2 4AT
Tel: 020 7240 3933

Candell Lighting Ltd, 20-22 Avenue Mews, London N10 3NP
Tel: 020 8444 5232

Flos Ltd, 31 Lisson Grove, London NW1 6UB
Tel: 020 7258 0600

GFC Lighting, Westminster Business Square, Durham Street, London SE11 5JH
Tel: 020 7735 0677

The London Lighting Co, 135 Fulham Road, London SW3 6RT
Tel: 020 7589 3612

Louis Poulsen, Surrey Business Park, Weston Road, Epsom, Surrey KT17 1JG
Tel: 01372 848800

Mr Light, 275 Fulham Road, London SW10 9PZ
Tel: 020 7352 7525

SKK, 34 Lexington Street, London W1R 3HR
Tel: 020 7434 4095

Wall materials and coverings

J W Bollom & Co and **Bollom Display**, PO Box 78, Croydon Road, Beckenham, Kent BR3 4BL
Tel: 020 8658 8672
• *felt, hessian, glass fibre, suede, metallic coverings, decorative paints*

Bruynzeel Multipanel UK Ltd, 4 Freebournes Court, Witham, Essex CM8 2BL
Tel: 01376 519924
• *plywood panels for cladding*

Fired Earth, Twyford Mills, Oxford Road, Adderbury, Oxfordshire OX17 3HP
Tel: 01295 814399
• *glazed wall tiles*

Focus Ceramics Ltd, Unit 4, Hamm Moor Lane, Weybridge Trading Estate, Weybridge, Surrey KT15 2SD

Tel: 01932 854881
• *glass blocks*

John Oliver Paints, 33 Pembridge Road, London W11 3HG
Tel: 020 7221 6466
• *colours mixed to order*

Luxcrete Ltd, Premier House, Disraeli Road, London NW10 7BT
Tel: 020 8965 7292
• *glass bricks and blocks*

World's End Tiles, Silverthorne Road London SW8 3HE
Tel: 020 7819 2110

Fabrics

Cath Kidston, 8 Clarendon Cross, London W11 4AP
Tel: 020 7221 4000
• *1950s retro-style fabrics*

Donghia UK Ltd, G23 Chelsea Harbour Design Centre, London SW10 0XE
Tel: 020 7823 3456

Ian Mankin, 109 Regents Park Road, London NW1 8UR
Tel: 020 7722 0997
• *plain natural fabrics, such as canvas, ticking, muslin*

Liberty, 214 Regent Street, London W1B 5AH
Tel: 020 7734 1234
• *Scandinavian-style, modernist fabrics*

Hard Flooring

Birmingham Art Flooring (UK) Ltd, 47 Formans Road, Sparkhill, Birmingham B11 3AR
Tel: 0121 702 2080
• *terrazzo, mosaic tiles*

Bragman Flett, Unit 4, 193 Garth Road, Morden, Surrey SM4 4LZ
Tel: 020 8337 1934
• *aluminium sheet flooring*

Delabole Slate, Pengelly Road, Delabole, Cornwall PL33 9AZ
Tel: 01840 212242

Gooding Aluminium Ltd, 1 British Wharf, Landmann Way, London SE14 5RS
Tel: 020 8692 2255
• *aluminium sheet flooring*

Mosaic Workshop, 1a Princeton Street London WC1R 4AX
Tel: 020 7831 0889
• *mosaics designed & made in glass, marble and ceramic*

Paris Ceramics, 583 Kings Road, London SW6 2EH
Tel: 020 7371 7778
(Yorkshire: 01423 523877)
• *English and French limestone, mosaic and ceramic tiles*

J. Preedy and Sons, Lamb Works, North Road, London N7 9DP
Tel: 020 7700 0377
• *design and install glass flooring*

Stone Age Ltd, 19 Filmer Road, London SW6 7BU
Tel: 020 7385 7954

The Reject Tile Shop, 196 Wandsworth Bridge Road, London SW6 2UF
Tel: 020 7385 9610
also
2 & 2a Englands Lane London NW3 4TG
Tel: 020 7483 2608
• *bargain supplier of ends of lines*

Wood Flooring

Davis Howarth Jacob,
8 St Albans Place,
London N1 0NX
Tel: 020 7704 0540
• *specialist joiners for
laying plywood floors*

Finewood Floors Ltd,
Unit 5, Gibson Business
Centre, R/O 800 High
Road, London N17 0DH
Tel: 020 8365 0222
• *wide floorboards,
strip and parquet in
hardwoods*

**The Hardwood
Flooring Co Ltd**,
146-152 West End Lane,
London NW6 1SD
Tel: 020 7328 8481
• *supply and installation of
new and reclaimed strip,
blocks, planks*

Junckers Ltd, Wheaton
Court Commercial Centre,
Wheaton Road, Witham,
Essex CM8 3UJ
Tel: 01376 534700
• *Danish producer of
solid hardwood flooring in
beech, oak and ash*

Kahrs (UK) Ltd,
Timberlane Estate, Quarry
Lane, Chichester, West
Sussex PO19 2FJ
Tel: 01243 778747
• *Swedish producer of
pre-laminated wood floors*

Lassco, St Michael's,
Mark Street,
London EC2A 4ER
Tel: 020 7749 9944
also
Maltby Street,
London SE1 3PA
Tel: 020 7394 2101
• *new and reclaimed
hardwood, stone and tile*

Walcot Reclamation, 108
Walcot Street, Bath, Avon
Tel: 01225 444404
• *Reclaimed wooden flooring*

Carpet and natural fibre flooring

Afia Carpets, Chelsea
Harbour Design Centre,
Lots Road, London
SW10 0XE
Tel: 020 7351 5858
• *rugs, fitted carpets*

**The Alternative Flooring
Company**,
Unit 3b Stephenson Close,
East Portway Industrial
Estate, Andover,
Hampshire SP10 3RU
Tel: 01264 335111
• *coir, sisal, seagrass, jute*

**Christopher Farr
Handmade Rugs**,
212 Westbourne Grove,
London W11 2RH
Tel: 020 7792 5761
• *contemporary rugs*

Crucial Trading Ltd,
79 Westbourne Park Road,
London W2 5QH
Tel: 020 7221 9000
• *natural fibre coverings*

Helen Yardley, A-Z
Studios, 3-5 Hardwidge
Street, London SE1 3SY
Tel: 020 7403 7114
• *designer of contemporary
rugs*

Roger Oates Design,
The Long Barn, Eastnor,
Ledbury, Herefordshire
HR8 1EL
Tel: 01531 631611
• *English flatweave rugs
and runners*

The Wilding Partnership,
The Malt House, Eardisley,
Herefordshire HR3 6NH
Tel: 01544 327405
• *designers and makers
of handtufted rugs and
carpets*

Linoleum, vinyl, leather and rubber flooring

**The Amtico Company
Ltd**, Epsom Business Park,
Kiln Lane, Epsom,
Surrey KT17 1DH
Tel: 01372 745 909
London showroom:
Tel: 020 7727 3560
• *vinyl flooring; design and
cutting service*

Bill Amberg, 10 Chepstow
Road, London W2 5BD
Tel: 020 7727 3560
• *leather flooring*

Dalsouple, PO Box 140,
Bridgwater, Somerset
TA5 1HT
Tel: 01278 727733
• *rubber flooring*

First Floor (Fulham) Ltd,
174 Wandsworth Bridge
Road, London SW6 2UQ
Tel: 020 7736 1123
• *Dalsouple rubber,
linoleum, vinyl, wood,
carpet, natural fibres*

Forbo-Nairn Ltd, PO Box
1, Kirkcaldy, Fife KY1 2SB
Tel: 01592 643777
• *linoleum, vinyl and
carpet tiles*

Litchfield Clare Limited,
16 Horselydown Lane,
London SE1 2LN
• *leather floor tiles*

Sinclair Till,
793 Wandsworth Road,
London SW8 3JQ
Tel: 020 7720 0031
• *linoleum, carpet,
natural fibre coverings,
wood flooring; custom
design service*

Plastics

**Hamar Acrylic
Fabrication Ltd**, 238
Bethnal Green Road,
London E2 0AA
Tel: 020 7739 2907

General information

Building Centre, 26 Store
Street, London WC1E 7BT
Tel: 020 7637 1022
• *displays building
materials and products;
information service*

Business Design Centre,
52 Upper Street, Islington
Green, London N1 0QH
Tel: 020 7288 6440
• *100 trade and contract
showrooms; regular
exhibitions*

Crafts Council,
44 Pentonville Road,
London N1 9BY
Tel: 020 7278 7700
• *promotes craftspeople;
regular exhibitions*

**Federation of Master
Builders**, Gordon Fisher
House, 14-15 Great James
Street, London WC1N 3DP
Tel: 020 7242 7583
• *16,000 members in
construction industry;
11 regional offices*

**Interior Decorators &
Designers Association
Ltd**, 1-4 Chelsea Harbour

Design Centre, Lots Road,
London SW10 0XE
Tel: 020 7349 0800
• *association of interior
designers, decorators and
trade suppliers*

**Royal Institute of British
Architects**, 66 Portland
Place, London W1B 1AD
Tel: 020 7580 5533
• *advice and information on
architectural practice*

Furniture and accessories

Aram Designs, 3 Kean
Street, London WC2B 4AT
Tel: 020 7240 3933

Castle Gibson, 106a Upper
Street, London N1 1QN
Tel: 020 7704 0927
• *secondhand utility fittings
and storage furniture*

The Conran Shop,
Michelin House, 81 Fulham
Road, London SW3 6RD
(and branches)
Tel: 020 7589 7401

Designers Guild,
269-277 Kings Road,
London SW3 5EN
Tel: 020 7351 5775

Egg, 36 Kinnerton Street,
London SW1X 8ES
Tel: 020 7235 9315

Habitat,
196 Tottenham Court Road,
London W1P 9LD
(and branches)
Tel: 020 7631 3880

Heal's,
196 Tottenham Court Road,
London W1P 9LD
Tel: 020 7636 1666

The Holding Company,
241-245 Kings Road,
London SW3 5EL
Tel: 020 7352 1600
• *home storage*

Ikea,
for branches
Tel: 020 8208 5607

John Lewis Partnership,
278-306 Oxford Street,
London W1A 1EX
(and branches)
Tel: 020 7629 7711

Lloyd Davies, 14 John
Dalton Street,
Manchester M2 6JR
Tel: 0161 832 3700

Muji,
for branches
Tel: 020 7323 2208

Nice House, The Italian
Centre Courtyard, Ingram
Street, Glasgow G1 1DN
Tel: 0141 552 2373

Purves and Purves,
220–224 Tottenham Court
Road, London W1T 7QE
Tel: 020 7580 8223

SCP, 135-139 Curtain
Road, London EC2A 3BX
Tel: 020 7739 1869
• *contemporary classics,
from Corbusier to Jasper
Morrison*

Themes and Variations,
231 Westbourne Grove,
London W11 2SE
Tel: 020 7727 5531

Tom Tom, 42 New
Compton Street, London
WC2H 8DA
Tel: 020 7240 7909
• *modern retro from the
1960s and 1970s*

INDEX

Page numbers in *italics*
refer to illustration captions

A

Aalto, Alvar 11, 100, 101,
103
aluminium
door panels 75, 76
staircase *21*
window treatment 83
Anglepoise lamps 112
Arts & Crafts Movement 6, 9
artworks *121, 123, 124, 134*

B

bareness *11,* 122-3
barriers, removal 11
baseboards, *see* skirting
boards
bathrooms
doors *77*
furniture and fittings
108-9, *109*
tiles *29, 30*
windows *73*
Bauhaus 9-10
bead curtains, against
doors *75*
bedrooms
new modern *6*
walls *25*
wood cladding *28*
beds, on wheels 126
birch plywood flooring,
project 68-9
blinds, window 80, *81,*
84-5, *84-5*
roller 84, *84*
Roman 84-5, *85*
Venetian 80, *81,* 85,
85, 89
boundaries, in open space 35
see also dividers
boxes, for storage *123*
Breuer, Marcel 7, 10, *60,* 100
bubblewrap, at windows 88
butcher's block tables 106

C

cabinets, filing 126-7, *127,*
138-9

calico 87, *88*
candles 134, *134*
canvases, painted *51*
project 40-1
carpets 47, 60-1, *60*
casters, *121,* 126, *126*
ceramic tiles
cladding 30
flooring 54
ceramics, on display *130*
chairs
bentwood café *100,* 101
functional 103
by Marcel Breuer 7, *60*
'space age' *99*
variety of 101
chaise longue by
Le Corbusier 7, *7,* 100
Chesterfield sofa *104*
cladding for walls 21,
27-30
clothes storage 125
clutter, avoidance *11,*
122-3
coir carpets and rugs 60,
61, *63*
colour
choice 22-3
to avoid clinical effect *13*
in concrete *31,* 57
curtains *82*
fashionable 23, *23*
furnishings 104
muted 24
necessity of 14
and painted walls 22
single colour schemes
23
strong 23, 24
variety 14
colourful canvases,
project 40-1
commercial premises,
converted 11
concrete
colour-washed *31,* 57
modern flooring 50,
56-7, *56*
polished *16*
containers, everyday 132
Coray, Hans,
aluminium chairs 103

Corbusier, Le 10, 100
chairs 16, 100, 101
chaise longue 7, *7,* 100
colour 8
stark windows 80
cornices 32, 33
corrugated metal *21*
cotton fabric 87, *87*
crafts, display of 132, *132*
cupboards *14, 123, 123,*
124-5, *134*
curtain rail *81*
curtains 80, 82, *86-8*
curves, in partition walls 37
curvilinear walls *24*
cushions 105, *105*
textured, project 114-15

D

detail, wall-decoration 32-3
dhurries 62
dining rooms/areas
wooden floors *49*
sliding doors *74*
display *see* storage and
display
dividers 34, 35, *37*
storage unit *124*
dividing screens,
project 38-9
dividing space 34-7
door handles 76, *77*
doors 73-7
'fluid' (bead/fabric) 74
glass 75, *75,* 76
movable 75
ribbon 74
sliding *73,* 74, 76,
77, 124
as strong features 74-5
drawers *124,* 125

E

Eames, Charles 100
eclecticism 11
ethnic style 131, *131*

F

fabrics
curtains 82, 86-8, *86-8*
geometric designs 86, *86*
stripes 86

textured 86
variety 86-7
fibre carpets 61, *61*
filing cabinets 126-7, *127*
mobile, project 138-9
fireplaces
stripped *32, 122*
unadorned *105*
fitted kitchens 106
fixtures and fittings 106-9
flexibility, in furniture 99
floorboards, painted,
project 64-5
flooring, birch plywood,
project 68-9
floors and coverings 46-63
carpets 47, 60-1, *60*
concrete 56-7, *56*
as dividers *52*
glass 57, *57*
hard 46
hard tiles 54, *54*
laying 49
leather 58
linoleum 47, 58-9, *59*
metal *47,* 56, 57
mosaic 55, *55*
natural fibres 61, *61*
rubber *58,* 59
rugs 62-3, *63*
stone 52-3, *52-3*
terrazzo 57
vinyl *58,* 59
wood 48-51, *48-51*
flowers, display of 16, 132,
132-3
'form follows function'
credo 9-10
Formica, in doors 77
Fornasetti style 27
frames for pictures 134
French windows 72
special glass for 79
fridges, coloured 107
frosted glazing,
project 90-1
functionalism 6-7
furniture and furnishings
98-113
details 110, *110*
early twentieth-century 10
fixtures and fittings 106-9

textured 86
variety 86-7
lighting 111-13
mixture *100*
as room divider *34*
soft furnishings 104-5
types 100-1

G

glass
coloured 79
frosted *79,* 90-1
as invisible barrier 11
opaque 78
shatter-proof 79
wired security glass
cladding 28
glass bricks *8, 35,* 36-7,
36-7, 54, 74, 77, 79
glass doors 75, *75,* 76
glass floors 57, *57*
glass panels, in doors 76
glass panes *10*
glazing of windows and
doors 78-9, *78-9*
glazing, frosted,
project 90-1
Gray, Eileen 62

H

hallways, modern *9, 31*
halogen lighting *107,* 112,
125
handles 110, *110*
hard tiles, flooring 54, *54*
hardboard tiling,
project 66-7
hardboard wall *28*
headings for windows 82-3
heating, underfloor *13*
high-tech 11, *56, 58*
humour 130

I

innovation 7
international style furniture
10, 98

J

Jacobsen, Arne 11, 100
chairs 8, 98, 101
Japanese influence
bathroom 108
interiors 129

Johnson, Philip, Connecticut
house 11
jute carpets 61

K

Karan, Donna 134
kelims 62
kitchen furniture 106-7,
106-7
kitchen store cupboards *99*
kitchen utensils 107
kitchenette, recessed *75*
kitchens *13*
floors *47, 52,* 55-6,
58-9
industrial style *47,* 125
suitability for modern
style 106
walls *21, 23, 34*
kitchens/dining areas *34, 36*
kitsch 88, 130, *130*
Knoll fabrics 86

L

laminated window
hangings, project 135
lamps 112, 113, *113*
lampshade, veneer,
project 136-7
Larsen, Jack Lenor 86
lava lamps 130
leather, in flooring 58
'less is more' 8, 122-3,
122-3
libraries 17
Liebes, Dorothy 86
light *6, 11,* 13, 80, 111
light shades 113, *113*
lighting 111-13, *110-13*
types 112-13
limestone floors *52,* 53
linoleum 47, 58-9, *59*
lockers 127
lofts, useful conversion
11, 12
Loos, Adolf 12
loose covers 104

M

machine aesthetic 6-7
Mackintosh, Charles Rennie
7, *25*

'maid-servers' 106
mantelpieces 122
Marriott, Michael, lamps
    113
Maugham, Syrie 25
MDF (particleboard)
    doors 75, 76, 77
    pelmets 83
    shutters 89
    storage 124, 125
metal
    corrugated *21*
    flooring *47, 56*, 57
    sheeting on doors 75
    shuttering 89
    skirting boards
        (baseboards) 33
metro-style tiling 30
Mies van der Rohe, Ludwig,
    chair 8, 100
minimal display 129
mirror glass, wall
    cladding 28
mirror mosaic, wall
    cladding 28
mix and match, furniture
    102-3
mobile filing cabinet,
    project 138-9
mobile storage 126
modernism
    creating a contemporary
        scheme 14-17
    criticism 8
    groundwork 12-13
    history 7-8
    themes and inspiration
        9-11
modernity 6-7
'modernizing' 12
monochrome treatment 14
mosaic
    bathroom *29*
    floors 55, *55*
    tiling in wall-cladding 28
mullioned windows 72-3
muslin for curtains 82,
    82-3, *87-8*

N

natural displays 132-3
natural fibre carpets 61, *61*

neoprene
    cushions 105
    in wooden strip
        flooring 48
New Modern 6-17
notice boards 134

O

old and new, mix 121, *121*
older property, modern
    interiors 12
opaque glass, frosted 78
open plan 11, 34-5
ornament 12

P

paint
    distressed on walls 24
    over tiles 106
    on walls *21, 23-4,*
        22-5
    on wooden flooring 51
painted canvases,
    project 40-1
painted floorboards,
    project 64-5
painted target, project 42-3
paintings *see* artworks
paper
    substitute for fabrics 88
    for walls 26-7, *27*
paring down *11*, 122-3,
    122-3
parquet flooring *47*
particleboard *see* MDF
pebbles as decorative
    feature *133*
pelmets 83
perfume in interiors
    16, 134
Perriand, Charlotte, chaise
    longue 100
Perspex (Plexiglas)
    picture frames 134
    shutters 89
    in storage 124, *124*
    table tops 101
    wall cladding 28
    window dressing 83
plaster, unpainted 30-1
plastics 11, 110, *124*
    cladding for walls 28

Plexiglas *see* Perspex
plumbing, bathroom 108,
    109
plywood 110, *111*
    cladding 27, 28
    doors 74, *74*
    flooring 51, 68-9, *100*
    moulded 10
    pelmets 83
    shutters 89
poles, for curtains *81, 82*
    variety 82-3
polyethylene
    corrugated in doors 77
    glazing 79
polypropylene 110
pop culture 130
portholes
    in doors 37, 76, 79
    windows 80
primitive style 131, *131*
putting away 123, *123*
PVC flooring 59

R

radiators 109, *109*
    freedom from *13*
reading room *17*
recycled furniture 98, 101
remodelling 12
re-use of materials 126-7
ribbon doors 74
roller blinds 84, *84*
    pull-up, project 92-3
Roman blinds 84-5, *85*
rubber flooring *58*, 59
rugs, 62-3, *63*

S

saloon doors 76
sanding wooden floors 50
scale
    in design 16
    of furniture 103
    playing with *128, 129*
Scandinavian design 11
scent in displays 16, 134
screens 35
    and dividers 16-17
    pivoting floor-to-ceiling
        75-6
    plastic *34*

seagrass floor coverings 61
sealing
    plaster 31
    wooden floors 50-1
sensuous displays
    134, *134*
shelves
    curved *131*
    kitchen *99*
shelves, drawers and
    cupboards 124-5
shoji screens 35
shop fittings 127
shutters 89, *89*
    window, folding, project
        94-5
sideboards 125
sisal carpets 60, 61, *61*
skirting boards
    (baseboards) 32, 33
slate floors *52, 53*
slate tiles with wood *52*
sofas 101, *101*, 103
soft furnishings 104-5
solar materials 88
solar power 73
space 12
    creating 16-17
    new view 10, 11
spaciousness *16*, 102,
    102, 103
stained glass 79, *79*
stains, for wooden floors 51
staircase
    open spiral *6, 33*
    with built-in storage
        drawers *124*
stairwell, wood and chrome
    rails *49*
Starck, Philippe 100
    bathroom fixtures 108
    lamp 113
steel
    flooring *56*, 57
    mesh, wall cladding 28
stone floors 52-3
stone walls *31*
stools, stacking 101, 103
storage and display 120-34
    mobile 126
    paring down 122-3
    putting away 123

storage units, as room
    dividers *104*
streamlining 10
stripping walls 30-1
sugar paper, at windows *78*

T

table top, revamped,
    project 116-17
target, painted,
    project 42-3
tea towels, at windows 88
terrazzo flooring *56*, 57
texture, in finishes 14, 16
Thonet, Michael, bentwood
    chairs 101
throws 105
tiles
    bathroom *29, 30*
    ceramic for cladding 30
    ceramic for flooring *54*
    hard, for flooring 54, *54*
    metro-style 30
    painted over 106
    wall cladding 28
tiling, hardboard,
    project 66-7
timber *see* wood
tracing paper, at windows
    78, 88
transformative furniture 101
trunks, on casters 126, *126*
tubular steel 10
tungsten lighting 112
Tyvek material 35

U

underfloor heating *13*
upholstery, wearability 105
utility fittings in the home
    11, 103

V

Velcro fastenings 104
veneer lamp shade,
    project 136-7
Venetian blinds 80, *81*, 85,
    85, 89
Victorian style 9, 10, 12
vinyl
    fabric 87-8
    flooring *58*, 59

sheeting over
    windows 78

W

wall displays 134
wall-hangings 40-1
wallpaper 26-7, *27*
walls 20-37
    cladding 21, 27-30
    curvilinear *24*
    detail 32-3
    painted *21*-5, 22-5
    sliding wooden panels
        35
    stone *31*
    'stopped short' *33*
    white 20, 24-5, *75, 103*
wardrobes 125
wash basin *109*
window treatments 80-1
windows 72-3
    indoor 37
    recessed *73, 85*
    wooden *49*
wire mesh 110
de Wolfe, Elsie 25
wood
    bathroom *29*
    cladding *26, 27, 28*
    finishes 48, 51
    flooring 48-51, *48-51*
    hardwood strip 48
    renovation 50
    solid strip 48
    species 48
wooden doors 77
work benches, kitchen 107
worktops and splashbacks
    106
Wright, Frank Lloyd,
    house *10*

Z

Zanotta see-through
    armchair 98
zinc
    in bathroom *29*
    cladding 28, 76
    floors 57
    storage 125
    table tops 101
    window treatment 83

ACKNOWLEDGMENTS

The authors would like to thank Denny Hemming, Helen Ridge, Tony Seddon and Rachel Davies for their enthusiasm and professionalism; and Jake Bowie for his help with the special projects.

The publisher would like to thank Liz Boyd for her assistance with picture research; and Margaret Doyle, David Lee, Angela Morris and W H Newson.

The publisher also thanks the following photographers and organizations for their kind permission to reproduce the photographs in this book.

1 Ray Main; **2** Chris Gascoigne (Simon Conder Associates)/View; **4** Chris Gascoigne (Stanton Williams)/View; **5** Ray Main; **6** Christoph Kicherer (Gary Tarn/John Pawson); **6-7** Henry Bourne (Architect: Robert Grace/Interior: Sarah de Teliga); **7** Verne Fotografie (Architect: Glenn Sestig); **8** Nick Hufton (Peter Bernamont)/View; **9** Peter Cook (Erich Mendelsohn)/View; **10** *above* Peter Cook (Frank Lloyd Wright)/View; **10** *below* Paul Ryan (Alias Design)/International Interiors; **11** Ray Main; **12-13** Simon Kenny/Belle Magazine; **13** Hotze Eisma; **14** Verne Fotografie (Architect: Glenn Sestig); **14-15** Dennis Gilbert (Rick Mather)/View; **15** Peter Aprahamian/Conde Nast Publications Ltd – House & Garden; **16-17** Vogue Living (Australia); **17-19** Ray Main; **20** *background* Richard Davies; **20** Verne Fotografie (Architect: Quatre Mains); **21** Simon Kenny Vogue Living (Australia); **22** *left* Verne Fotografie (Architect: Stijn Peeters & Partners); **22-3** Ray Main; **23** Ornella Sancassani; **24** James Mortimer/Conran Octopus; **25** Ray Main; **26-7** Mads Mogensen; **27** Dennis Brandsma/vt wonen; **28** Ray Main; **29** *above* Mads Mogensen; **29** *below* James Mortimer/ Conran Octopus; **30** Ray Main; **30-1** Gionata Xerra; **31** Paul Ryan (Bernardo Urquita)/International Interiors; **32** Peter Cook/View; **33** Chris Gascoigne/View; **34** Alexander van Berge; **34-5** Ray Main; **35** Nick Hufton (Peter Bernamont)/View; **36** Ray Main; **36-7** James Mortimer/ Conran Octopus; **37** Dennis Brandsma/vt wonen; **44-7** Ray Main; **48** Robert Sledziewski/Eigenhuis & Interieur; **49** *above* Peter Cook/View; **49** *below* Paul Ryan (Hariri & Hariri Architects)/International Interiors; **50** Nicholas Kane/Arcaid; **51** Hotze Eisma; **52** Johnathon Pilkington/Homes & Gardens/ Robert Harding Syndication; **52-3** Ray Main; **53** Verne Fotografie (Architect: Dirk Coulleit); **54** *above* Trevor Mein (John Wardle)/Arcaid; **54** *below* Alan Weintraub/Arcaid; **55** *above* Paul Ryan (Kathy Moskal & Ken Foreman)/ International Interiors; **55** *below* Trevor Mein/Belle/Arcaid; **56** *above* Peter Aprahamian (Nico Rensch); **56** *below* Gionata Xerra; **56-7** Alexander van Berge; **57** Ray Main; **58** Simon Kenny/Belle/Arcaid; **58-9** Paul Ryan (Paula Pryke & Peter Romanuk)/International Interiors; **59** vt wonen; **60** *left* Verne Fotografie (Architect: Glenn Sestig); **60** *right* Geoff Lung/Belle Magazine; **61** Hotze Eisma; **62** *below* Susana Bruell; **62** *above* Dennis Gilbert (Rick Mather)/View; **63** Nick Pope/Options/Robert Harding Syndication; **70-1** Ray Main; **72** *background* Henry Wilson (Ian Dew)/The Interior Archive;

72-3 Ray Main; **73** Trevor Mein (Andrew Parr)/Belle/Arcaid; **74** Alberto Piovano (P. Zanella)/Arcaid; **75** *above* Verne Fotografie (Architect: Marcussi); **75** *below* Ray Main; **76-7** Nick Hufton (Peter Bernamont)/View; **77** Tim Goffe (Tim Bushe Associates); **78** Georgia Glynn Smith/Elle Decoration; **78-9** Ray Main; **80** Trevor Richards/Homes & Gardens/Robert Harding Syndication; **80-1** Dennis Gilbert (Charles Eames)/ View; **81** Ray Main; **83** Verne Fotografie (Architect: Dieleman & Debo); **84** Ray Main; **85** *above* Hotze Eisma; **85** *below* Ray Main; **86-7** Paul Wiering/Eigenhuis & Interieur; **86** Gilles de Chabaneix (Sty; Catherine Ardouin)/Marie Claire Maison; **87** Ray Main; **88** Paul Wiering/Eigenhuis & Interieur; **89** *above* Ray Main; **89** *below* Belle Magazine; **96-7** Ray Main; **98** *background* Ray Main; **98-9** Ray Main; **99** Verne Fotografie (Architect: Glenn Sestig); **100** Andrew Twort/World of Interiors; **101** Christoph Kicherer (Gary Tarn/John Pawson); **102** Peter Cook/View; **103** Simon Upton (Sue Skeen)/World of Interiors; **104-5** Ray Main; **105** Hotze Eisma; **106-8** Ray Main; **107** Ray Main (sdh interiors) **109** *above* Hotze Eisma; **109** *below* Chris Gascoigne (Gerrard Taylor Associates)/View; **110** *left* Simon Brown/The Interior Archive; **110** *right* Chris Gascoigne/View; **111** John Best/Australian House & Garden; **112** Ray Main; **113** *above* Paul Wiering/Eigenhuis & Interieur; **113** *below* Inside/Met Home; **118-19** C. Simon Sykes/The Interior Archive; **120** *background* Eigenhuis & Interieur; **120-1** Paul Ryan (Albert Turrick)/International Interiors; **121** Mads Mogensen; **122** Ray Main; **122-3** Verne Fotografie (Architect: Glenn Sestig); **123** Hotze Eisma/vt wonen; **124** *above* Michael Mack; **124** *below* Trevor Mein/Belle Magazine; **125** Verne Fotografie (Architect: Cousse & Goris); **126** Hotze Eisma; **127** Eigenhuis & Interieur; **128** Ray Main; **129** Chris Gascoigne (Gerrard Taylor Associates)/View; **130** *above* Jean-Francois Jaussaud (F. Dostal); **130** *below* Simon Brown/ Conran Octopus; **131** *left* Francis Amiand (Stylist: Gafi Reyre)/Marie Claire Maison; **131** *right* Simon Brown/The Interior Archive; **132** Peter Aprahamian/Conde Nast Publications Ltd – House & Garden; **133** *left* Ray Main; **133** *right* Nick Pope/Options/Robert Harding Syndication; **134** Ray Main.

Every effort has been made to trace the copyright holders, architects and designers. We apologize in advance for any unintentional ommission and would be pleased to insert the appropriate acknowledgment in any subsequent edition.

The photographs on the following pages were taken specially for Conran Octopus by Hannah Lewis: **38-43, 64-9, 90-5, 114-17, 135-9**